Keeping Kids Safe

For Cierra Frances, my granddaughter, my 5-year-old wonder; my joy.
May you always be passionate, confident, and safe. — PT

To my mother, Estelle, who started me out in life with lots of "heart touches."
To my dear friend and mentor, Pnina, who helped me to name them.
To my husband, Herb, who is never stingy with his; and to the children . . . may they learn
to create a world where "heart" touches abound. — SLK

Ordering

Trade bookstores in the U.S. and Canada please contact:

Publishers Group West
1700 Fourth Street, Berkeley CA 94710
Phone: (800) 788-3123   Fax: (510) 528-3444

Hunter House books are available at bulk discounts for textbook course adoptions; to qualifying
community, health-care, and government organizations; and for special promotions and fund-raising.
For details please contact:

Special Sales Department
Hunter House Inc., PO Box 2914, Alameda CA 94501-0914
Phone: (510) 865-5282   Fax: (510) 865-4295
E-mail: ordering@hunterhouse.com

Individuals can order our books from most bookstores, by calling **(800) 266-5592,**
or from our website at **www.hunterhouse.com**

KEEPING KIDS SAFE

A Child Sexual Abuse Prevention Manual

Second Edition

Pnina Tobin, M.P.A., and Sue Levinson Kessner, M.S.

Hunter House PUBLISHERS   CPL

Hunter House Inc., Publishers
PO Box 2914
Alameda CA 94501-0914

Library of Congress Cataloging-in-Publication Data
Tobin, Pnina.
Keeping kids safe curriculum : a child sexual abuse prevention manual / Pnina Tobin and Sue Levinson Kessner.—2nd ed.
p. cm.
Originally published: Montreal : Learning Publications, c1990.
Includes index.
ISBN 0-89793-333-8 (cl) — ISBN 0-89793-332-X (pb)
1. Child sexual abuse—United States—Prevention—Handbooks, manuals, etc. I. Kessner, Sue Levinson. II. Title.

HV6570.2 .T63 2001

372.17'86—dc21   2001016618

PROJECT CREDITS

Cover Design: Jinni Fontana
Book Design and Production: Jinni Fontana
Photographer: Joan Bobkoff
Photos of Posters: Scott Braley
Copy Editor: Bevin McLaughlin
Proofreader: Lee Rappold
Acquisitions Editor: Jeanne Brondino
Associate Editor: Alexandra Mummery

Editorial and Production Assistant: Emily Tryer
Sales and Marketing Assistant: Earlita K. Chenault
Publicity Manager: Sara Long
Customer Service Manager: Christina Sverdrup
Order Fulfillment: Lakdhon Lama
Administrator: Theresa Nelson
Computer Support: Peter Eichelberger
Publisher: Kiran S. Rana

Printed and Bound by Data Reproductions, Auburn, Michigan
Manufactured in the United States of America

9 8 7 6 5 4 3 2 1   Second Edition   02 03 04 05 06

Table of Contents

Important Note

The material in this book is intended to provide a review of information regarding child abuse prevention. Every effort has been made to provide accurate and dependable information. The contents of this book have been compiled through professional research and in consultation with health-care professionals. However, health-care professionals have differing opinions and advances in medical and scientific research are made very quickly, so some of the information may become outdated.

Therefore, the publisher, authors, editors, and professionals quoted in the book cannot be held responsible for any error, omission, or dated material. The authors and publisher assume no responsibility for any outcome of applying the information in this book.

Acknowledgements

The programs and curricula contained in this manual are based on the Children's Self-Help Project—a pioneering child sexual abuse prevention program based in San Francisco, California. For almost 15 years, this organization was responsible for developing and disseminating a unique model of prevention for children, teens, families, and communities throughout the United States.

This manual is the product of the efforts of many individuals and groups who provided the soil upon which the seeds of our prevention philosophy grew. Others provided nutrients and watered the seeds frequently. Still others shaped, trimmed, and pruned the programs until they grew to fit the needs of different ages, abilities, and ethnic groups in both rural and urban populations.

The authors would like to thank the following people and organizations for their unique contributions:

Sally Cooper and the Child Assault Prevention Project (CAP) of Women Against Rape, Columbus, Ohio, for their pioneering work in the development of an inspirational prevention model that includes a profound respect for children.

Cordelia Anderson and the Illusion Theater of Minneapolis, Minnesota, for brilliantly modeling the use of theater in teaching children to discriminate among touches, a previously taboo subject.

Julie Robbins, Becky Balsam, and Sarah Thompson, who joined Pnina Tobin in 1981 to develop the philosophy and original CSHP curricula for elementary, junior high, and high school students.

Mariana Valdez, former CSHP staff member, who joined the project in its infancy, bringing her expertise in early childhood education and genuine caring and love for kids. Mariana worked tirelessly over the years as a role model and trainer for new staff and volunteers.

Tanya Russell, former CSHP staff member, who came to us during the project's childhood. She used her analytical thinking and clear perceptions in the fine-tuning of the curricula and training programs.

To the staff and many volunteers of the former CSHP, who imparted the philosophy of respect for children while adding their own unique presentation styles.

We are indebted to our colleagues and mentors in the field—Sandra Butler, Cordelia Anderson, Carol Plummer, Geraldine Crisci, Barrie Levy, and Esta Soler—for their validation of prevention theory and their faith in its use in the prevention of child sexual abuse.

We are grateful to the California Coalition Against Sexual Assault (CALCASA) for providing us with the opportunity to work together again, on the revision of our manual, after a 10-year period of going in separate work directions. This work represents a joyful revisiting of our collaboration, a deepening of our friendship, and a reaffirmation of our commitment to the field of prevention.

We want to also acknowledge Hunter House for publishing the revised edition of *Keeping Kids Safe* and affording us the chance to reach many more people with our message.

And, finally, from the bottom of our hearts, we thank the many thousands of children and teens who have already benefited from and who, we believe, will emerge empowered from the *Keeping Kids Safe* experience. It is our hope that they and their families will have an impact on this and the next generation, as they raise a less vulnerable population of children.

"Heart" touches to you all!

PNINA M. TOBIN
SUE LEVINSON KESSNER

Introduction

This manual contains two sections: **Facilitator's Guide** and **Curricula.**

The **Facilitator's Guide** contains background information on child sexual abuse, with particular emphasis on the dynamics of incest and other sexual abuse and their effects on the child. It contains a discussion of the philosophy of and need for primary prevention, and specific strategies used by *Keeping Kids Safe* in preventing sexual abuse. Prevention Educators will find it helpful as they work with young children to reinforce key personal safety concepts. By *Prevention Educators,* we mean those who work with children in a prevention role, such as children's advocates, teachers, health-care workers, parents, and child-care workers, or anyone else interested in learning how to keep kids safe. Libraries and resource centers will also want to use this manual as a valuable source of reference.

Several "How-To" sections are included as well. Prevention Educators are supplied with guides for setting up and implementing the complete *Keeping Kids Safe* program, from initial workshops for school personnel and parents to the age-appropriate classroom workshops for children. These guidelines are based on the experience of concerned educators in developing, modifying, and presenting these programs. Detailed outlines for parent and school staff workshops are included, and may be used at these workshops until the presenter has familiarized him- or herself with the contents.

Hints for working with school systems and successful classroom management techniques are provided. Guidelines for conducting Private Time, a specified time for children to talk with adults individually after each presentation, are included. Suggestions for successful intervention on behalf of victims are also included. Information on reporting child abuse and working with the child protection system is supplied as well. Forms that have been found helpful for recording information before, during, and after school presentations are provided. Finally, for those interested in pursuing the issue further, a bibliography of books, videos, audiotapes, and videotapes on the subject of sexual abuse is included.

The **Curricula** section contains detailed, word-for-word curricula for the two-session Early Childhood and Elementary School workshops. These pages may be used as scripts for classroom presentations until the new presenter has memorized them. Each session has been subdivided into lessons, with objectives and stage directions for each included in the margins. These lessons can be used in sequence or as separate modules, to allow greater flexibility for presenters.

Additional Programs and Materials

In addition to elementary and early childhood programs, curricula and training are available in the following areas:

Middle School prevention curriculum: for students ages 11 to 14.

High School prevention curricula: one is to be used by a team of adult presenters; the other, a peer education program, trains teenagers to present the program (with adult supervision) to their peers.

I'm Somebody—Child Sexual Abuse Prevention Curricula for Children with Disabilities: programs for children with developmental, visual, physical, learning, and emotional disabilities.

Keeping Kids Safe: Family Activity Booklet: personal safety games and exercises for the whole family.

An order form for supplemental materials used in the *Keeping Kids Safe* program, including puppets and song tapes, can be found at the end of this book.

Part 1 — Facilitator's Guide

1

Why Prevention?

Child Sexual Abuse—An Overview

The information in this section and the sections that follow may be condensed and used in workshops with parents, teachers, health workers, and the community at large.

Child sexual abuse is forced or manipulated touching or sexual activity between an adult and a child or even an older child and a younger child. Sexual abuse includes sexual activities such as peeping, flashing, and child pornography, in addition to sexual intercourse, sodomy, and mouth-to-genital contact.

The sexual abuse of children and teens is a critical problem in our society. It is estimated that one in three girls and one in seven boys are sexually abused before they reach the age of 18! Children with disabilities are seven to ten times more at risk for abuse than their nondisabled peers.

Child sexual abuse is a violation of adult authority and trust as well as of the law. Although it is commonly believed that a need for sex is the primary motivating factor, other social, cultural, and personal factors may come into play. In many cases, the offender is motivated by a need to feel powerful, coupled with a preference for, as well as access to, children.[1] The costs, both monetarily and psychologically, to victims, their families, and society are high. Child sexual abuse produces teen and adult problems such as alcoholism, drug addiction, prostitution, suicide, and runaway behavior.

Contrary to popularly held beliefs, children are abused most commonly by someone known to them. In at least 85 percent of the cases, the offender is a trusted adult—a family friend, teacher or other caregiver, neighbor, parent, stepparent, grandparent, or other relative. These adults, or older children,

[1] David Finklehor, *Sexually Victimized Children* (New York: The Free Press, 1979).

typically gain the child's trust by developing a "special" relationship with her; they desensitize her to affectionate forms of touching, and, at some point, "cross the line" from nurturing to abusive touch. Secrecy is usually involved. The touching usually occurs in private, without witnesses, and often the child is threatened into keeping the abuse "our special secret." When there is a trusting, loving relationship between the two, sometimes the threat of withdrawal of love from the child is enough to ensure secrecy.

INCEST

Sexual abuse of children by other family members, or those in a surrogate parental role, is commonly known as *incest.*

Stepfather- or father-daughter incest is the most commonly reported offense. Over 95 percent of offenders in reported incest cases are male. In addition to fathers, reported offenders also include uncles, brothers, and grandfathers. Incest families often appear normal, while the heavy burden of the secret of incest rests primarily on the child, who knows or suspects that her family is not really normal.

Physical violence and bodily harm are rare in intrafamilial sexual abuse. What is more common is that the child is *tricked* into sexual acts with the relative and the nature of the contact progresses, from touching or fondling to mouth-to-genital contact and sometimes full intercourse over a period of years.

Most incest victims love and trust their abusers. Offenders often manipulate this sense of love and trust and violate the child's expectation of love and protection from a trusted adult. Thus, when the abuse begins—usually between the ages of 4 and 6 years—the child is, understandably, very confused. Adding to the child's confusion is the fact that the sexual acts may feel "good"; the body may respond with pleasure though there also may be a

sense that something is wrong. The confusion is heightened when the child is told that these interactions must be kept a secret. Usually, interactions that are "okay" are not hidden.

CHILDREN

Children in incest families often provide caretaking functions for adults doing an inadequate job of caring for them, including care of the home, shopping, cooking, and meeting the sexual needs of the offending parent. Incest victims tend to have strong feelings of responsibility for keeping their families together. Typically, they are told that if the secret of incest is revealed, the family will fall apart, Daddy will go to jail, or Mommy will have a nervous breakdown. The implication is that the abuse is their fault and their responsibility.

It is important to be aware that children rarely lie about sexual abuse. If anything, they tend to withhold information or minimize it. Children lie to get out of trouble, not to get into it. Often they keep the secret of sexual abuse for years. Then, at some point during adolescence, when the abuser puts more pressure on the child and the child wants more freedom to be with peers, the truth comes out. It is difficult for children and adolescents to talk about abuse because they are afraid of punishment, of family rejection, of breaking up the home, and of not being believed.

The child or adolescent often senses there is something "wrong" in the special relationship, but cannot find the words to articulate what it is. She may feel she causes the problem by her "bad" behavior and may blame herself or worry about being punished. (Often, the offender takes advantage of this by telling the child that she "makes" him behave this way.) Because the relationship is often affectionate and may be the only source of affection in the child's life, the child may wish to keep it a secret to protect her source of affection.

Many victims blame themselves for not stopping the abuse, especially when it takes place over a long period of time. As a result, they feel a tremendous sense of guilt, and it can be highly traumatic to relive the experience through the retelling.

Perpetrators often claim that children are sexually provocative. While children may be curious and excited about their own and other people's bodies, that does not mean they are seeking sex with adults or older adolescents. They are seeking attention, affection, and acceptance, and look to adults to provide safe limits within which these needs can be met. Children do not invite abuse.

The effects of intrafamilial sexual abuse are numerous and deep. A pervasive sense of low self-esteem, depression, and "differentness" from other kids causes victims to have difficulty relating to others socially. Some victims mask their problems for years; this does not mean they do not experience pain. Unless these children can be helped to feel safe and valuable, and are given the opportunity to work through the abuse, they are likely to experience problems in later life.

MOTHERS

Mothers of incest victims often do not know (consciously) that sexual abuse is taking place in their family. A variety of factors prevent or discourage them from becoming aware of the abuse or taking action if they do know about it. Commonly, the mothers are emotionally and financially dependent on their husbands and feel powerless. Often, they themselves were victims of childhood sexual abuse or are currently abused by their husbands, so their own low self-esteem and fear causes them to worry about whether they'll be believed, get support, or have the ability to stop the abuse or leave the abusive situation. Like the child victims, they fear they'll be blamed and criticized (e.g., for

being a "bad" mother) rather than understood and protected. Mothers of incest victims are likely to minimize or deny suspicions of abuse or even disbelieve their children if and when they are told. The incest mother's inability to take action is a perfect match for the offender's denial that he is doing anything wrong.

OFFENDERS / INTRAFAMILIAL ABUSERS

Sexual abusers come from all walks of life and all social classes. The majority of abusers are seen by the community as "regular guys," and sometimes "pillars of the community." Inside their families, these men are often tyrannical and authoritarian. A large percent are over 25, of average intelligence and education, and tend to be conservative churchgoers. Many have problems with alcoholism. They are often immature and self-centered in their personal relationships. While they have strong needs for intimacy, it is often difficult for them to express their needs appropriately to their mates. They find it easier to reach out to their children for intimacy, support, and sexual gratification.

Not surprisingly, many offenders are found to have been abused as children. However, unlike female abuse victims, who often reenact their victim role in later life, males tend to identify with the original abuser, deny their own victimization, and then become abusers themselves. This reenactment of the abuser role may give them a temporary sense of power and control, the very things they were robbed of as child victims. Their denial and rationalization of the abuse leads them to label their own behavior as part of a loving "special relationship" or even as "teaching their daughter about sex."

Many of these men are charming and manipulative, masking their own fear and inadequacy. Their outward appearance allows them to seem more healthy and "together" to the community and in the courtroom than the mother and child, who are, understandably, shaken, confused, and distraught about the abuse.

Like the mother and the child, the offender needs an adequate, appropriate response from the community, including the legal system. He obviously is not in control of his behavior. For the protection of the child, the abuse must be stopped. For the abuser's well-being, he must be shown that his abusive behavior is totally unacceptable. Only then can he begin the treatment process. Without adequate legal intervention, he may continue the sexual abuse. Therefore, the legal system must monitor the offender until such time as there is a reasonable hope that he has accepted responsibility for his actions, gotten in touch with the underlying motives for his behavior, and found some effective means of controlling his impulses—either by himself or with ongoing professional help.

LONG- AND SHORT-TERM EFFECTS

Child sexual abuse can be extremely harmful. The child may isolate herself from peers and others who could help her, because she thinks she is the only one who has ever experienced abuse. To escape or numb the pain, she may:

- retreat into a fantasy world,

- "split" into good and bad selves,

- evidence self-destructive behavior (be prone to accidents, eating and sleeping disorders, poor school performance),

- engage in adolescent high-risk behavior (truancy, running away from home, drug and alcohol abuse, promiscuity, threaten or attempt suicide).

As a late adolescent and adult, she may:

- experience difficulty in intimate relationships,

- feel valued only as a sex object,

- be affected in her work life, either by spending long periods of time underemployed or unemployed, or by making work her entire life.

With therapy and support, many survivors of incest and other sexual abuse are able to engage in full, productive lives. **No one, however, survives this experience without some scars.**

Myths and Facts

Myth: Most people who sexually abuse a child are strangers to the child.

Fact: Seventy-five to eighty-five percent of abusers are known to and trusted by the child.

Myth: Child sexual abuse is physically violent.

Fact: Most of the time children are molested by being manipulated, flattered, or talked into the abusive acts. Although sometimes violence (to the child or to other family members) is threatened, sexual abuse is most often **not** physically violent.

Myth: Children who are abused act seductively, or "ask for it" by dressing seductively.

Fact: Children often "test out" sex roles with adults by acting or dressing "seductively." Children, no matter what age, are not "asking for it." It is the responsibility of the adult to set physical and emotional limits.

Myth: Most people who sexually abuse children are low-income or unemployed minorities.

Fact: Sexual abusers come from all racial, ethnic, class, and economic backgrounds.

Myth: Most people who sexually abuse children are gay men.

Fact: Ninety-five percent of all abusers are males who are heterosexual in their choice of adult partners. (The assault of a young boy by a male offender is most often not a homosexual act.)

Myth: Men who are "horny" or lacking a sexual partner are the ones who sexually abuse children.

Fact: Most abusers have consistent sex partners and are "getting enough" sex. Often offenders say they don't "get enough" to rationalize the abuse.

Myth: If intercourse did not occur during the molestation, the child will not be traumatized by the abuse.

Fact: Children are emotionally traumatized by abuse, even if no intercourse occurs.

Myth: Brother-sister incest is not as serious as adult-child incest.

Fact: Recent research on brother-sister incest reveals the effects of this incest as being as severe as adult-child incest. Some research indicates brother-sister incest is more physically violent.

Myth: If children are molested it is because they were left unsupervised by neglectful parents (or single parents).

Fact: Many children are molested while being supervised by a parent or other caregiver (at family gatherings, in crowded elevators and buses, and by the caregivers themselves).

Myth: Mothers in incest families often know about the incest but do not protect their children.

Fact: Mothers are most often surprised when the incest is disclosed. In some instances they may have an intuitive feeling that something is "wrong" with the father-child relationship, but do not know about the incest.

The Need for Prevention

All children are potential victims of sexual abuse. Where sexual abuse is concerned, there are no sex, age, socio-economic, or racial barriers. National estimates are as high as 250,000 cases per year. Some research indicates that at least one in three girls and one in seven boys are molested before reaching the age of 18. A recent study by Diana Russell states that 38 percent of 900 women interviewed had been sexually assaulted before the age of 18.

Most children are not molested by "dangerous strangers" in dark alleys, as is commonly assumed. The fact is that at least 85 percent of the time, children are molested by someone they know and trust (a family member, friend, or neighbor). Well-intentioned parents warn their children about strangers, yet are often at a loss when it comes to protecting them from people they know and trust.

Public interest in the issue of child sexual abuse and the need for prevention in the community is at an all-time high. Parents are becoming increasingly aware of the need to teach their children ways to prevent potential assaults and avoid or diminish their long-term effects. Since child sexual abuse is rapidly becoming a familiar household word, parents are less frightened of programs that **talk to children directly**

about this sensitive subject. In fact, many parents are relieved to learn of the existence of such programs, since they are often at a loss as to how to educate their children.

Children are extremely vulnerable to sexual abuse because of their trust in and total dependence on adults, and their lack of information regarding the real dangers of molestation. Parents cannot supervise children 24 hours a day to protect them. Even when parents believe they have entrusted their children to a reliable adult, abuse may still occur. It is crucial, therefore, to educate children early so they feel strong enough to resist abuse themselves or to get adult help in doing so.

WHY PREVENTION?

The effects of childhood sexual abuse are very costly, both economically and psychologically, and the effects are long-lasting. Sometimes people don't recover. Abuse affects one's sexuality, intimate relationships, and lifestyle. When the "acting out" behavior of teenagers (e.g., truancy, promiscuity, prostitution, drug addiction, delinquency, running away, suicide attempts) is questioned, experts find that these behaviors are often the direct result of sexual abuse. Treatment is costly. The cost to society of adolescents' delinquent behavior is high.

Cycle of abuse: Many molesters were abused as young boys (81 percent in one study). Many women survivors of incest unconsciously choose men who will molest their children. Interviews with adolescent offenders have brought to light evidence of their own victimization as children.

Parents cannot always protect their children from molestation. They usually can't supervise their children 24 hours a day. Even if they could, they might not be able to protect them. Also, the assumption that parents can protect their children through supervision plays into the myth of the "dangerous stranger" as the usual perpetrator of sexual abuse. In fact, parents and caretakers cannot always be trusted to protect their children because they themselves may be the abusers!

The "lock 'em up and throw away the key" method doesn't work to prevent sexual abuse. The costs of incarcerating and rehabilitating these social outcasts are prohibitive. Not only that, many are released only to again commit the same crime against children. Child molesters are not easily "cured."

Treatment is necessary and important for victims. Yet, if we are really going to stop sexual abuse, we must get at the underlying causes or the cycle of abuse will continue.

By doing prevention now, we may have a great impact on the future. We must work to educate and change a society that supports and condones the abuse of women and children.

WHEN WE DO CHILD SEXUAL ABUSE PREVENTION,

- we make connections between ads that objectify and exploit women and children and child sexual abuse and incest

- we remind people that the traditional ways boys and girls are raised in our society (males to be aggressive, to not take "no" for an answer; females to be passive and to look to others for protection) contributes to their risk of abusive and victim behavior later in life

Prevention work that focuses only on potential victims and their families is short-sighted. At the same time we address ourselves to potential victims, we need to address the root causes of abuse in our violent and sexually exploitative society. Only then can we have an impact on this generation and generations to come.

Philosophy and Prevention Strategies

Parents sometimes ask if teaching child sexual abuse prevention means we are going to teach sex education to their children. Our answer is that we teach sexual abuse prevention; that sexual abuse is an abuse of power that uses sex as its vehicle. Even when no actual force is used, we're talking about someone who often has parental rights, who is usually twice as big as the child, and who manipulates the child's need for affection. In this context, even a vague threat of force being used against him or her can leave the child feeling helpless.

PREVENTION STRATEGY

Our prevention strategy seeks to correct the imbalance between adults and children by empowering children in the following ways:

Information. Information is power. We teach children the realities of child sexual abuse and dispel commonly held myths. We teach children that they own their bodies and have the right to choose when, how, and by whom they are touched.

Self-esteem building. Research reveals that children are more vulnerable when their self-esteem is low. The offender plays on the child's neediness, promising affection and high valua-tion in exchange for sex. By reminding children that they have a right to say "no" and applauding their efforts at skill-building, we help them raise their self-esteem.

Self-defense skills. We teach children physical and mental self-defense skills. We provide children with a repertoire that includes a self-defense yell and other physical strategies, as well as some assertiveness techniques such as saying "no," getting help, and running away.

Resources. To reduce the vulnerability caused by the child's isolation, we encourage children to expand their network of trusted adults.

Children Have Intuitive Power

Have you ever noticed that sometimes when a baby or young child meets someone for the first time, he or she acts frightened or cries? It may be that the child intuitively feels uncomfortable about that person. Yet we well-meaning adults talk the child out of his or her feelings. We say, "Don't cry, that's my friend (or brother, etc.)." Intuitive feelings are not encouraged or nurtured in a young child. Our child abuse prevention program tries to tap into this intuitive power, which we call "funny feelings." We encourage children to use their intuition—to trust their funny feelings about someone and protect themselves from the potential molester.

A question asked of us is, "Do children really have an intuitive sense?" Yes, we believe they do. We need only think about times in our own childhood when we had funny feelings to realize that children have them. We may remember "knowing" what a person was really like even though our parents told us to like him or her. Children express these funny feelings physically because they often don't have words to conceptualize them, and so rarely can talk about them.

Linda Sanford, in her book *The Silent Children: A Parent's Guide to the Prevention of Child Sexual Abuse,* writes about a child's "inner voice" or intuitive sense. Whether it is experienced as a little voice, a feeling in the pit of one's stomach that danger is near, or as "radar," children do experience funny feelings. It is up to us to acknowledge they exist, and to reinforce children's paying attention to, talking about, and acting on these feelings.

Trusting Intuition

Trusting their intuition can be a powerful tool for children to use in preventing sexual abuse. First, the feelings can serve as an early warning signal to children that "something is wrong with this picture." For example, when an older person acts friendly but stands too close to the child, if the child gets a funny feeling because the person is intruding on her body space, she may get out of the situation before it becomes abusive.

Second, paying attention to his or her intuitive feelings can be a strong boost to a child's self-esteem. After receiving repeated positive reinforcement for trusting their feelings, including being believed and helped, children begin to feel that they can trust this "inner voice" and can help themselves keep safe. Besides learning that they are able to keep themselves safe, children also learn when a problem is too confusing and they need adult help.

Validating Intuition

Finally, children are learning to use their other senses to help them validate their intuition. For example, many parents ask, "Is my child going to be afraid when I kiss her goodnight after she's in this program? Will she be fearful of all adults?" No; we believe children learn to collect visual, auditory, and tactile cues to help them. When a parent kisses the child goodnight and acts sneaky or nervous, asks the child to keep it a secret, and French kisses her, the child usually adds these clues up and "feels funny." When a parent is behaving appropriately, kissing the child in a friendly and open manner without the veil of secrecy, the child feels fine.

Sensory Cues

In our workshops we work with children to help them describe all the sensory cues—visual, auditory, and tactile—that may contribute to funny feelings. For example, we ask children about role-players' body language and facial expressions. ("What was her face saying about the touch?") We also discuss bribes offered by potential offenders. ("Was ten dollars a lot of money to pay for moving a few cartons?") In answering these questions, children have shown us that they combine information received through all five senses to back up funny feelings.

So, if your child tells you about a funny feeling, believe her or him. Your support can go a long way towards protecting and empowering your child.

In conclusion, every child has the right to a safe childhood, free from the horror of incest or other kinds of sexual abuse. We believe this very strongly. Whenever possible we prefer that the offending parent be removed from the family and that the child-and-mother unit be supported.

Children have a right to correct information about when, where, and by whom they are at risk of being abused. We teach children that it is not only the "dangerous stranger" who may be sexually abusive, but that even someone in their family might force or talk them into unwanted touching. We support their right not to keep secrets about unwanted touch, even when it involves someone they love or who loves them. We know the long-term effects of keeping incest a secret are extremely debilitating and we confront this issue directly and honestly in our classroom skits.

Our Philosophy in the Classroom

Our philosophy regarding respectful adult-child communication underlies our prevention approach in the classroom:

Children own their bodies and minds. We respect their right to set their own boundaries and to define their body space. We show our respect and don't invade their space. For instance, we don't pinch them on the cheek as a greeting. Many adults don't realize the size advantage they have over small children and will stand over them, forcing them to look up. With small children in our program, we sit or kneel at their level so we can connect with them. We also seat them in a semicircle, thus avoiding the "us" and "them" feeling of traditional classroom seating arrangements.

Children have a right to say "no" to unwanted touches and to tell someone if they feel their body space is being invaded. This includes saying "no" to adults who the child has been taught to obey. We tell children, "If someone tries to touch you in your private parts, you can disobey the adult and say 'no.'" Automatic obedience to adults makes children too vulnerable.

In our presentations, we give children, from preschool up, a chance to say "no" to an abusive babysitter, uncle, etc., role-played by a puppet or a presenter. The children get reinforcement from each other and valuable practice in asserting their right to decide how and by whom they are touched.

How We Model Respect for Children in the Classroom

The following are some of the ways we model respect for children:

We listen when they talk. Respect for children includes listening to them when they talk to us about their problems.

We don't expect them to use adult vocabulary and we try to use their experiences, their words, and their pictures in our classroom presentations.

We don't judge children's responses. We don't use the word "right." It implies there is a "wrong." We avoid using "That's a good answer." It implies that other answers are bad. When adults judge, they set themselves up as all-knowing, all-powerful people, which can be intimidating to young children learning to be more assertive. An alternative to a judgmental response might be "Okay, yes, thank you." Such responses acknowledge the uniqueness of a child's answer, yet allow room for all children's responses to be correct.

We avoid teasing children or putting them "on the spot." For example, if a child forgets his or her answer when called on, our nonjudgmental approach is again evident: we give the child time to think, and, if a response still is not forthcoming, we tell the child we'll get back to him or her when he or she remembers.

We use nonjudgmental descriptions. When we show children posters of offenders or victims, we avoid using derogatory words to describe the people. For example, children often describe people who are different from them as "strange," "weird," or "funny-looking." We focus instead on neutral descriptions—or simply point and say, "someone who looks like this."

We reframe children's answers into more neutral descriptive responses. For example, if a child says, "Queers do it," we say, "Often people think it's only gay men who sexually abuse children."

We emphasize that there's no one "right" way to keep safe. Each child must find the ways that work for him or her.

We emphasize that sexual abuse is never the child's fault. In this way we are teaching children not to judge themselves harshly if they are abused. Judgments, whether positive or negative, are detrimental to the child's self-esteem.

There are ways in which Prevention Educators can raise children's self-esteem. First: show the child how he or she is unique and special. Rewarding differentness instead of belittling it can go a long way. Rewarding specific behaviors can also be a strong self-esteem booster: "I liked the picture you painted" is more effective than "Good girl."

RESPECT SHOWS

Respect for children shows in our approach to classroom management.

We set ground rules. We tell children we will move them if they are disruptive, but no one is removed from the classroom. We believe children aren't "bad" if they disrupt the presentation; they might just be having a hard time hearing the information. (Disruption may be an indicator of distress or sexual abuse, and it is important for the child to stay in the group unless he or she is extremely noisy.) The observer may stand behind a disruptive child and touch him or her lightly on the shoulder in order to refocus his or her attention.

Respect for children includes taking their feelings and ideas seriously. Our interactive format allows presenters to listen to children's ideas for keeping safe and to their success stories.

We encourage dialogue and do not presume to know all the answers.

We don't "talk down" or condescend to children. For example, if a child expresses fear of being alone with a specific relative or caregiver, we take this fear seriously as a possible indicator of sexual abuse. Adults often minimize these fears or try to talk a child out of having them.

We trust children to use this information to protect themselves. We present children with a repertoire of skills, from basic assertiveness skills to doable self-defense. When we do this, the message is, "We trust you to use these skills when needed—but if you don't, and you get abused, it's not your fault." We prefer this trusting message to ones that include many "don't"s. "Don't"s transmit a lack of trust. Using them says to children that we are afraid they won't be able to think for themselves or use their own judgment in a scary situation. "Don't"s can be a challenge to a child to rebel against adult authority by breaking rules. Thus, well-intentioned parents may get the opposite of the wished-for effect from rules and "don't"s.

We respect children's ability to trust their own intuition about uncomfortable situations involving strangers or known adults. However, respecting children does not mean telling them they can solve all their problems themselves. That would be unrealistic as well as disrespectful. Teaching children to be totally independent is just as unrealistic as teaching them to be totally dependent. Neither one works all the time. Sometimes children need help stopping abuse and reporting it to authorities. Sometimes the adults a child turns to for help in difficult situations are precisely the ones who cannot be trusted, because they are either denying the truth of the molestation, or are the perpetrators themselves. Children can be taught to use their intuition in finding trustworthy adults when they need help.

We believe children rarely lie about sexual abuse. They may be confused about times and places or tell stories to protect the offender and their "secret." Believe children when they report sexual abuse and support them through the reporting process. Sexually abused children need to have their reality validated and to be told they are blameless for the abuse.

We teach children to keep on telling until they are believed. In that way children can get help to stop any abuse that might be occurring. We also give them cards printed with the telephone numbers of places to get help. They are encouraged to call and get help if they need it.

SUMMARY

We believe in a primary (before the fact) prevention effort, focused on children and supportive adults in their community, as well as on changing the environmental conditions that foster the exploitation of young children.

**The importance of direct contact with children as a focus of the prevention effort can- *not be stressed enough. As we mentioned above, the secrecy surrounding abuse by a trusted adult is particularly difficult for young children. It may contribute to their isolation, guilt, and self-destructive behavior. Our prevention effort focuses on breaking the silence by correcting misinformation, informing children of their rights, encouraging them to say "no" in uncomfortable interactions with adults, and teaching them to get help from people they trust. The parents of the children we work with are targeted as well. Parents may warn their children about strangers, but may not realize the importance of protecting them from relatives, neighbors, and other familiar adults. Parents also need training in believing and supporting children when they report.*

Teachers are in a unique position to support children and impart prevention information to them. Training teachers helps them provide clear information to children. It also encourages them to believe and support disclosing children and to report suspected cases of sexual abuse.

A prevention program cannot exist in isolation. It must strive to educate the entire community by increasing the community's awareness of the societal conditions supporting child sexual abuse. Educational presentations should be made to health professionals, community service groups, religious groups, and the media. Efforts should be made to point out the societal conditioning of males as exploiters and of females as sex objects. Media interviews should be granted in order to reach a broader audience. The community needs to hear about the number of male victims who have become offenders and the number of female victims who continue to be abused.

Our goal is to reduce children's vulnerability to all kinds of abuse. However, we are attempting to empower children in a society that sees children as little love objects or as nonpersons. We are doing our work at the same time that the media is portraying adolescents as seductive, nubile sex objects, thereby giving permission to adults to use and abuse them for their own satisfaction. Some adults may use these media images to rationalize their behavior, saying things such as, "She wanted it—she seduced me." This makes our work more of a challenge, requiring as it does that we reeducate people about the nature of sexual abuse.

However, true primary prevention doesn't stop with public education. We must advocate for change in a society that until recently has not actively sought to eliminate sexual abuse. Everyone benefits when children are less vulnerable to abuse. Even those without either children or a history of abuse in their past will benefit. The psychological, social, and financial costs involved in investigation, prosecution, and treatment in cases of sexual abuse will be greatly reduced when children learn to protect themselves. *An ounce of prevention truly is worth a pound of cure!*

Why Children Are Vulnerable

Children are totally dependent on adults, both physically and emotionally. Adults may take advantage of this dependency by threatening the withdrawal of physical or emotional support, or by manipulating the child's need for affection.

Adults are more powerful, physically and psychologically. An adult can usually physically overpower a child. Even though many adults do not use physical force to coerce a child into sexual abuse, the knowledge that the potential to do so exists may be used as a threat. An adult might say, "Do this with me or I'll beat you up" or "If you tell, I'll hurt you."

Children believe the myth of the "dangerous stranger." Children are taught to avoid being in dark alleys, taking candy from strangers, or getting in a car with an unknown adult. Recent research reveals, however, that over 85 percent of the time, children know and often trust their molester. He is often a relative or friend of the family. Children, then, while looking out for strangers who look and act odd or different from them, are unprotected 85 percent of the time.

Children believe the myth that molesters are from low-income, uneducated families and are usually from a culture or ethnic group other than their own. Due to the rampant racism in our society, it is the minority offender who is most often incarcerated or otherwise punished for his offense, while many upper-middle-class white men go unpunished. Children, then, are vulnerable to approaches by traditionally "respectable" middle-class whites.

Children believe the myth that child sexual abuse is always violent. This leaves them vulnerable to more subtle, less violent verbal manipulation and coercion by trusted adults.

Children are taught blind obedience to adult authority. Since many children are raised to "listen to your grandpa" or "do what your babysitter says," they are left vulnerable to those caregivers who would talk them into sexual abuse. Not all adults are trustworthy. To reduce children's vulnerability, we need to add this caveat: "Obey adults unless they want to touch you in a way that makes you uncomfortable."

Children are isolated from community support. They are not taught to use friends and trusted adults as supporters and allies. The secrecy surrounding sexual abuse and the threat of punishment for revealing the secret isolate children further from those who could help stop the abuse.

Children often are not believed when they try to disclose abuse. This is especially true when the child is under 7 and/or has few verbal skills, or when the offender is "respectable" (for example, when he is a clergyman). Children's stories are often minimized, discredited, or attributed to a "vivid imagination." Not believing children when they try to report abuse leaves them more vulnerable.

Children often have low self-esteem. All children, by virtue of their dependent, second-class status with respect to adults, feel "not good enough." Therefore, any adult can easily prey on a child's need to feel unique, valued, and special. Children are susceptible to these approaches, especially if they feel they are not valued by those closest to them. Children with disabilities may feel they are a burden to their families and caregivers, and may comply with an adult's wishes in order not to make trouble. Also, since children often blame themselves for various family problems, they may blame themselves for causing the abuse, thus lowering their self-esteem further.

Girls are especially vulnerable to sexual abuse. Girls are conditioned to rely on adult males—primarily their fathers and, later, their husbands—for protection. Young girls are rarely taught to be self-reliant, to trust their own feelings, to be assertive, or to appreciate their own femaleness (to love themselves). Girls, like women, are objectified sexually in movies, television, ads, and other media; this subtly conditions them and encourages their use for sexual purposes.

Children believe the myth that sexual abuse rarely happens to boys. Boys, too, are conditioned in ways that leave them vulnerable to sexual abuse. Teaching boys that "real" men or boys don't cry or look to others for help creates a situation wherein boys who are molested are less likely to ask for help, lest they be seen as "sissies." Also, due to rampant antigay attitudes among children, many boys are afraid that if their molester is male, they must be gay (especially if they felt any sexual pleasure during the molestation). This fear makes boys less likely to report abuse. If a boy is molested by a woman, a double standard applies. Boys are conditioned to consider themselves lucky to learn about sex from an older woman. The subtle pressure to maintain silence increases their vulnerability.

Reducing Children's Vulnerability

HOW THE *KEEPING KIDS SAFE* PROGRAM WORKS

There are three components to our program:

- a parent workshop

- teacher in-service training

- a children's workshop

Contact with our program is typically initiated by a parent, principal, or group leader. Faculty and parent workshops are scheduled at this time, usually 1 to 2 weeks prior to a children's workshop.

Teachers participate in an in-service training workshop for a half-hour to an hour. They are instructed regarding their role and responsibilities before, during, and after the children's workshop in their classroom. Teachers learn to recognize signs of abuse, to assist children in disclosing abuse, and to support children and serve as advocates for their needs during the investigation process.

Parents are invited to participate in a 1- to 1½-hour workshop held at least 1 week prior to their child's workshop. Parents are trained in child sexual abuse issues, prevention exercises to use at home with children, and "do"s and "don't"s to follow when a child discloses. Parents are then asked to give permission for their child to attend the workshop.

Children's workshops are held in two sessions, 30 minutes to an hour each, on 2 consecutive days. Presentations are given by a team of two or three trained staff and/or volunteers.

PROGRAM HIGHLIGHTS

Session 1

On the first day, we define sexual abuse and body safety in language the children can understand. For example, the elementary school curriculum defines sexual abuse as "forced or tricked touch to private parts of your body or the other person's body." We identify the private parts of the body. The children are told that sexual abuse can happen anywhere, at any time of the day or night, and to any child, rich or poor, black, brown, or white. We also stress that all kinds of people can sexually abuse children. They may be strangers or people the child knows. In this way, we dispel myths children commonly believe about child sexual abuse. We also identify three special body rights that all children have:

- the right to be safe,

- the right to say "no,"

- and the right to ask questions about touches.

Next, we discuss touches that children like ("heart" touches), and dislike ("no" touches), and those touches that are confusing ("?"

touches). Presenters do four to six skits designed to illustrate various kinds of touches. With preschool and early elementary school children, colorful, child-sized puppets are used to illustrate and identify touches. Older children identify the touches themselves by voting.

In line with our philosophy of never leaving a child in a vulnerable position, each skit identified as a "?" or "no" touch is replayed, using children as actors and getting suggestions from the class. Skills suggested by the class and presenters are already in children's repertoire of behavior; they include running away, saying "no" or "stop," and telling someone they trust about the touch (getting help). It is extremely empowering for children to be able to practice prevention skills with their peers in preparation for real-life situations. Since many children blame themselves for abuse, we emphasize repeatedly that **if a child cannot stop a touch, it is *never* the child's fault.**

We sing our "Touching Song"(Appendix F) with both younger and older children to illustrate the three kinds of touches. Each verse is acted out with puppets, adults, or children to reinforce safe-keeping skills.

Session 2

The concepts presented during Session 1 are reviewed and expanded upon during Session 2. We introduce the concept of intuition or funny feelings—the "inner voice" in each of us that warns us something is about to happen. We believe children can employ this internal warning system as another tool to keep themselves safe. Age-appropriate skills are used to show children how they can use their funny feelings. Once again, children replay skits using safety suggestions from presenters and the class. Presenters also discuss bribery and give children practice in stranger identification in order to prepare them for possible stranger molestation. Children learn how to do a self-defense yell—a low-pitched, loud yell from deep in the diaphragm, which can be used to warn adults that the child needs help or to scare away the potential molester.

Finally, since children are most often molested by someone they know, we include a sequence on incest. Children are shown an initial approach to a daughter by the father, the reaction of an unbelieving mother, and a scene in which the child is believed and gets help. Children are taught new skills to help them deal with the more subtle manipulation by a caretaker or family member. Children are involved in the final skit of this sequence, in order to practice newly acquired skills and internalize them for future use.

Private Time

At the end of each session, we offer children a chance to ask us questions and clear up confusion about touches. This portion of the program is called "Private Time" and usually takes place in the 30 minutes immediately following the presentation. We are available to interact with the younger children on a one-to-one basis, reviewing what to do to keep safe and who to tell.

Children who have already experienced abuse may approach presenters for help at this time. Children may also go to their parents or teachers for help after the presentation. (Please see the section on child advocacy for a more in-depth discussion of conducting a one-on-one session with a child.)

2

Child Advocacy and Successful Intervention

Child Development Issues

THE EARLY CHILDHOOD CURRICULUM

The curriculum used with children ages 3 to 7 (enrolled in preschool through second grade) has been specifically designed to take into consideration the developmental needs and abilities of young children. Recognizing that very young children have a limited attention span, we repeat and reinforce key concepts on both days of the presentation. Children have ample opportunity to hear the concepts, recite them back, and hear them again. Since children in this age group usually ask for only the information they need—no more and no less—the curriculum allows the children to guide the presenters on how much information they can take in. Thus, it can be adjusted to meet the needs of each age and development level. Additionally, because children this age are at a concrete stage of development, in which they are able to use logical thinking processes but are not yet thinking abstractly, the three key concepts below are presented in a developmentally appropriate manner.

1. identification of private parts of the body

2. saying "no" to unwanted touches

3. telling someone they trust

We do not require children this young to do abstract brainstorming or thinking. Instead, we give them information in a clear and simple manner that they can understand. To meet the children's need for movement and their desire to do things for themselves, the curriculum includes experiential exercises, role-plays, and frequent stretch breaks, as needed. *Keeping Kids Safe* workshops for young children allow children to practice and integrate information through their individual involvement. Care is taken to assess the group's attention level and to limit the presentation to 30 or 45 minutes, depending on the age and concentration abilities of the children.

Puppets

Colorful, child-size puppets are used in the early childhood curriculum to help children attend to the sensitive material. Young children find puppets nonthreatening, and their bright colors help to engage the children and focus their attention. The use of puppets also helps to portray touches in a clear, demonstrative way.

Songs

Songs are introduced on both days to further clarify the concepts of the three kinds of touches and intuition (funny feelings).

Visual Aids

Visual aids (posters in primary colors) are utilized as well, to teach children the concept of safety and the facts of sexual abuse.

Language

The early childhood curriculum provides a language to explain sexual abuse to very young children, as well as a framework that offers youngsters a context in which to place sexual abuse. In this way, it lays a basic foundation that parents and teachers can build on and use to expand understanding, concepts, and language. The curriculum presents prevention information in a matter-of-fact manner. It gives children permission to talk about this sensitive issue with their family and teachers. Finally, the early childhood curriculum is not culturally bound; its intention is to be value-free, based on the recognition that we live in a pluralistic society that embraces a variety of cultures and social values.

THE ELEMENTARY SCHOOL CURRICULUM

The Elementary School Children's Workshop showcases our core curriculum. Its concepts and structure provide the basis for all other *Keeping Kids Safe* children's workshops. It is designed to be used with children age 8 to 11 years, in the third through fifth grade. (Note: Some second-grade classes are developmentally ready for this curriculum as well. Consultation with the teacher prior to the workshops is recommended to determine which curriculum will be most appropriate.) Children in this age group comprise a large range of developmental levels. In general, school age children have access to more information than the adults around them know or wish to admit. Children's degree of independence and self-reliance is usually directly related to their age, but in our world of instant multimedia exposure, children may come in contact with a lot of information that they cannot comprehend.

Involvement

Children of this age group tend to be much more involved and interactive with their peers than are younger children. Also, older elementary school children are able to integrate information instantly on many different levels, employing their sight, hearing, and intuition simultaneously to understand nonverbal interaction.

Brainstorming

Elementary age children learn best when given the opportunity to grapple with new concepts in their own individual style, brainstorming solutions for themselves, and then testing out these solutions in a safe environment.

Discussion

Though school age children (especially those in the upper grades) may test the adults around them to see if they are listened to, believed, and respected, we have found children at this level are eager to talk about sexual abuse when a supportive atmosphere is provided. Not only are they excited about meeting new people, but they are also stimulated by a chance to talk about a subject that confuses them, yet is generally off-limits to discussion. Many elementary school children have had some experience with or know something about sexual abuse. Perhaps they have heard about a local kidnap victim on the news, or watched a TV show that dealt with the issue. Maybe a friend or relative has had a personal experience with abuse. And some children have experienced sexual abuse firsthand, ranging from an obscene phone call to an abusive touch to their private parts. Most children who participate in *Keeping Kids Safe* workshops are looking for a context in which to decipher and assimilate the barrage of information they receive from the world around them about abusive situations.

Flexibility

The child abuse prevention information taught in the elementary school curriculum is presented in a nonthreatening, matter-of-fact, and flexible format that is accessible to all age levels, from the youngest to the oldest grades. Its open-ended, question-and-answer structure allows children to start at their own developmental level and build on skills and information they already have.

Our technique of asking, "What would you do to keep safe in this situation? Who would you tell?" allows the children to think for themselves, processing and using the information in their own way and in their own time.

Role-Playing

The role-playing portion of the curriculum provides a model of safe-keeping behavior and then offers a chance for students to practice the skills being taught. By role-playing themselves, or watching their peers role-play, they receive hands-on experience in preventing unwanted touches. This is a powerful learning tool.

The Curriculum

The elementary school curriculum offers children a chance to integrate and internalize the information they've learned—as well as an opportunity to talk to parents and teachers about it—before going to a deeper level on the second day. Thus, the curriculum gives children the language, structure, and permission to put child abuse in a context that is meaningful to them. As is the case with the early childhood curriculum, the school age presentations are not culturally bound; they teach children that anyone can sexually abuse a child and that all children are potential victims of abuse. The curriculum is presented in a value-free atmosphere in which all ideas and attitudes are encouraged.

Indicators of Child Sexual Abuse

Sexual abuse in children manifests itself in a number of ways, physically, behaviorally, and socially. The following list contains the common signs or indicators of child sexual abuse. Please note that these are general signs of distress and could apply to other problems. However, if any of these indicators exist, especially in combination, it is important to acknowledge the possibility of child sexual abuse and seek help.

In general, trust your intuition, even if there is no concrete physical evidence. If you have a funny feeling that a child has been sexually abused, based on your observations of the child, trust it. Reasonable suspicion of sexual abuse can be reported to your local child protective service agency or law enforcement agency. Phone numbers for these agencies can be found in the local telephone directory.

GENERAL BEHAVIORAL INDICATORS

- Sudden changes in behavior (fears/phobias, or extroversion to introversion)

- Disturbed sleeping patterns (nightmares, fear of sleeping alone)

- Changes in relationships to adults (avoiding a specific person)

- Problems in school (dramatic change in academic performance; difficulty concentrating; arriving early/leaving late; truancy; bullying peers and younger children; disrupting class)

- Withdrawal from friends/family

- Running away

- Inappropriate and obsessive sexual awareness and sex play; instructing or initiating sexual behavior with peers or younger children; seductiveness

- Drug/alcohol abuse

- Depression

- Low self-esteem; critical of self; unable to defend self

- Fear of being left with caregiver(s)

- Child states an adult is bothering her or him

- Compulsive masturbation

- Lack of friends; lack of trust in others; isolation from peers; discomfort with or extreme sensitivity to physical contact or touch

- Friends who are several years older

- Discomfort about undressing in front of peers

- Child suddenly acquires new, unexplainable toys, money, clothes

- Loss of developmental gains, regression to more childish behavior

- Fear of previously enjoyed places/people; fear of men or women in general

- Engagement in "acting out" or delinquent behaviors

PHYSICAL INDICATORS AND PHYSICAL SYMPTOMS IN YOUNG CHILDREN

- Complaints of headaches, stomach-aches, and overall not feeling well

- Physical ailments: pain in stomach or in anal or genital area

- Recurring vaginal or bladder infections

- Oral, genital, or anal bleeding

- Redness, swelling, itching, or trauma to the genital/anal area

- Bloody, torn, or stained underpants or diapers

- Pain when sitting or exercising; pain during urination or defecation

- Presence of sexually transmitted disease (STD/HIV)

BEHAVIORAL SYMPTOMS IN YOUNG CHILDREN

- Altered activity level

- Appearance of "seductive" behavior

- Sexual expressiveness—in play, speech, or drawings—that is inappropriate to age

- Clinging to one parent/fear of the other parent

- Regression to bed-wetting or thumb sucking

- Taking excessive baths

- Compulsive masturbation

- Refusal to take underwear off when undressing

- Not wishing to be left with caretaker(s)

- Radical change in behavior: fears, phobias, hypersensitivity, compulsions, withdrawal, depression

- Child says an adult is bothering him or her

- Inappropriate sleeping arrangements

- Peer and school problems

- Excessive curiosity about sexuality

- Inappropriate responses to strangers or acquaintances (overly fearful, overly friendly)

- Marked difference in behavior when parent is present/absent

- Retreating to fantasy world

- Appearance of retardation

- Eating or sleeping disorders

Classroom "Red Flags"

"Red flags" are behaviors or statements by children in the classroom during *Keeping Kids Safe* presentations that may or may not be indicators of sexual abuse or other problems. In response to "red flag" behavior, the presentation team should ask the classroom teacher or principal about the specific child, to put the behavior in context. The child in question should be encouraged to come to Private Time. If the child doesn't want to participate in Private Time, the presentation team leader should indicate to the appropriate staff member what the "red flag" behavior or statement might mean and encourage school site personnel to follow up with the child after the presentation.

RESPONSIBILITY

It is not our job to determine the exact significance of the "red flag." Our responsibility is to believe children and report reasonable suspicion of abuse.

"Red Flags" Include

- Sophisticated, knowledgeable, detailed, or specific answers. Example: When asked where sexual abuse happens, a child immediately responds, "In your bed when you're home with just your dad, at night."

- Falling asleep

- Falling out of chair

- Getting up and leaving room

- Being overly anxious to participate

- Refusing to participate at all during class

- Rocking motion or curling up in fetal position

- Continuously touching themselves in private parts (masturbation)

- "Super kid" syndrome. Example: A child responds to the question, "What would you do if someone tried to force or trick you into touch in your private parts?" with "I'd beat him up," "I'd karate chop him," or "I'd knock him out!"

- Raises hand continuously and then "freezes" or forgets question

- Inability to sit and listen

- Being overly attentive; goes to the extreme of keeping class quiet in order to hear

- Inappropriate wearing of heavy clothing (perhaps ashamed of body)

- Wanting to talk in Private Time but neither having anything to say nor wanting to leave

- Change in behavior from one day to the next or from one section of the presentation to the next

- When asked, "Who could you tell?" answers, "No one" or "I don't know."

- Dealing with specific aspects of the curriculum insistently. Example: "Where can it happen?" "But what if it's the child's fault?"

- Obsessive "what if?"s that no answer will satisfy

- Looks down/won't make eye contact with anyone

- Looks sad/depressed, unchildlike (i.e., too mature for age)

- Extreme lack of body space boundaries or requires too much personal space. Example: The child may cling to the observer or lean into or touch the child in the next seat during the presentation. Or he or she won't let anyone within touching range; seems to have an "invisible shield" around her- or himself.

Private Time

. . . .

Private Time is offered after each lesson for pre-school through second graders, and following the last session of the elementary school work-shop. (If time allows, it is ideal to offer Private Time after each session for older elementary children as well.) This segment of the program lasts up to one half hour each day. The ration-ale behind Private Time is to give individual chil-dren the opportunity to ask a question, share an experience, or clear up any misunderstandings they have about the material covered in the presentation in a safe, supportive atmosphere. The nature of Private Time differs in preschool/ early elementary and older elementary settings.

PRIVATE TIME FOR YOUNG CHILDREN

Setting/Structure and Questions to Ask

We have found that young children benefit from a less structured, free playtime either indoors or on the playground. The presenters and observer circulate among the children, asking questions from the curriculum to reinforce the body safety concepts:

- Do you know what a "heart" touch is? A "no" touch? A "question mark" touch?

- What can you do to keep safe if you get a "no" or a "?" touch?

- What can you say? Who can you tell?

- Can you point to your private parts?

- Do you get "heart" touches? "No" touches? "Question mark" touches? Can you tell me about them? Who gives you "heart" touches?

- If a child answers that they get "no" or "?" touches, ask: Can you show me, on your body, where you get those touches? Who gives you "no" touches?

Asking open-ended, nonleading questions in a relaxed and familiar setting also gives young children a chance to approach us with questions or concerns of their own.

Behavioral/Symbolic Cues

It is unusual for very young children to be able to clearly verbalize an incident of abuse in a one-to-one counseling setting. They are more likely to demonstrate their discomfort behav-iorally, during or following the presentation. Some examples of "red flag" behavior might be: curling up in a fetal position, "tuning out" or turning away from the presentation, or mastur-bating. They also may speak symbolically about abuse. One 4-year-old girl told her teacher she had a stomachache. Following our presenta-tion, upon direct questioning, we discovered that she had been molested by her babysitter's son. Children at this age often associate the stomach with the genital area.

Anatomically Correct Dolls

The use of anatomically correct dolls is a bene-ficial tool in helping a young child to talk about an abusive situation. It is easier for children of this age to point to body parts on a doll to show where they were touched (or asked to touch) by their abuser than it is for them to make a clear, concise statement, such as: "He touched me down there with his pee-pee."

It is appropriate to do further questioning with the child in a prearranged quiet place in the following situations:

- When a child exhibits "red flag" behavior during the presentation

- When a child is brought to the presenter's attention by a concerned teacher

- When a child responds affirmatively to the Private Time question, "Do you get any "no" or "?" touches?" (and indicates that these touches occur to his or her private parts).

The anatomically correct dolls can be used at this time to determine where, by whom, and how the child is being touched. It must be noted that the use of anatomically correct dolls has become controversial in recent years. There are some professionals in the field who believe their use can lead children to make disclosures. Because of this, you may consider alternatives like regular dolls, life-size puppets, or drawings of children and adults. Stuffed animals are not recommended, however, because they are not anatomically correct; they make it too easy for children to distance themselves from the reality of abuse perpetrated by a human adult.

Start by saying, "These are special dolls because they have private parts on their bodies, just like you and me. Can you point to your private parts? Can you find the private parts on the dolls' bodies? Let's pretend this doll is you. Is anybody touching you in your private parts in a way you don't like? Can you show me on the doll where you're being touched? Can you tell me who's touching you?" (If the child can say who or if it's a male or female, child or adult, pick up the appropriate doll.) "Let's pretend this is the person who touches you/touched you. Can you show me what happens/happened? Show me where he or she touched you. What part of the body did he or she use? Did he or she touch you over or under your clothes?"

While getting information from the child, it is very important to stress what a fine job they are doing, how brave they are to tell, that it's not their fault, and that you're going to help to get the touching to stop. It is also essential to ask nonleading questions. Asking open-ended questions and using the child's own words enable you to stay on track and to avoid the trap of "putting words in the child's mouth."

Other Methods to Aid Disclosure

One other method to aid disclosure, when anatomically correct dolls are not available, is to draw stick figures on paper (using large crayons) and ask the child to show you where and by whom he or she is being touched. Anatomically correct pictures can also be used, as can regular dolls and puppets. However, most children at this age don't have the conceptual skills to draw a "story" of what happened.

Another way to discover how a child is being touched is to use the Body Part Identification Game. You can make a nonthreatening game of disclosure by using the anatomically correct dolls or a hand-drawn picture of a person (front and back) to label the parts of the body, in the child's own words, and to determine if the child knows each part's function. You can start with the hair and ask, "What's this called?" and "What's it for?" Proceeding from extremities to other parts of the body and finally to the private parts, without judgment, creates a safe climate in which the child may feel comfortable enough to disclose an abusive incident. It also allows the presenter to learn the child's own words for the private parts. Use of the child's language can create a sense of familiarity and can be helpful in obtaining a clear, accurate disclosure from the child. Once you know the child's words for the parts of the body, you can ask the child to show you and tell you just where and how they've been touched.

When You Don't Have Enough to Report

Perhaps more often than we'd like, it is possible to leave a school without enough solid information to make a report to the authorities (i.e., who touched the child, where on the body the child was touched, when the child was touched, whether the child was forced to touch the adult, where the incident took place), even after every effort to uncover what happened has been made.

Yet a presenter may still have a strong feeling that something has happened to this child. It is important to remember, at these times, that through our prevention presentations we're giving children the language and permission to talk about sexual abuse. We are planting the seeds of assertiveness. This groundwork may enable a child to verbalize the incident at a later date, with ongoing support and encouragement from the child's teachers and/or family members. A preschool child may feel more comfortable disclosing to a known, trusted adult in his or her world. Thus, it is essential to share funny feelings and unanswered questions with the appropriate contact person at the school, for future follow-up.

Clearing Up Confusion about Touches

Some preschoolers and young school age children may verbalize confusion about:

1. spankings

2. doctors' exams

3. baths

All involve touches to private parts of their bodies that children typically do not like.

It is possible to clarify their confusion by saying:

1. "Sometimes adults (like Mom or Dad) may touch children on their bottoms in a way that children don't like, when children misbehave or do something they're not supposed to do. But if a big person hits you on your bottom and other places on you body real hard, and leaves marks, and it seems like they don't know when to stop, it's important to tell someone about it."

2. "Sometimes a doctor needs to look at our private parts to see if they're okay or to take our temperature. These are okay touches. Are Mom and Dad there when the doctor touches you? Does the doctor tell you not to tell anyone?"

3. "Sometimes moms and dads may need to help children keep clean by washing them in their private parts. Sometimes kids don't like baths, or they like to wash themselves. Does anyone touch you like that when you are bathing? Do they tell you not to tell anyone about the touch? Do they keep their hand on your private parts for a long time? Do they ask you to touch them? All kids have to take baths, even though you may not like them. But if you think you can wash yourself, can you tell your mom or dad that you'd like to try it by yourself?"

Most children, through intuition, and the cues an adult gives them, know whether a touch feels "okay" or "not okay." Children often know more than we give them credit for. That is why it is so important to believe children—even very young children—when they try to tell us about "no" or "?" touches.

ELEMENTARY SCHOOL PRIVATE TIME

Structure/Set-Up

A predesignated "private" place should be identified in each school, with enough space for two or three presenters to sit in different sections of the room with individual children. A faculty room, nurse's office, or unused classroom all provide privacy and lack of interruption. However, in schools with limited space, stairwells, hallways, and closets have all been utilized for Private Time. If the schedules coincide, the teacher may decide to take the rest of the class out to recess while the classroom is used for Private Time. If the presentation is held in a "neutral" room (i.e., library, auditorium, activity room), Private Time can be offered there as well.

At the end of the last session of the presentation, the concept of Private Time is explained to the children, and names of children who wish to participate are written on the board and on the Observation/Presentation Form. "Red Flag" children may also be asked discreetly if they wish to come to Private Time, but no child should feel forced to do so.

Children's names should be called from the top of the list (unless a child needs to leave early), and assigned to an available presenter. Chairs (one for each presenter and a child) should be set up before the children are called. Each set of chairs should face one another, several feet apart, and should be far enough away from the other presenters' chairs to prevent children from overhearing their classmates' questions and concerns. Presenters should have a Private Time Form to use in keeping a brief record of what each child said. Date, classroom number, teacher's name, and time of presentation should be entered at the top of the form. Detailed accounts of what a child said are necessary in the following situations:

1. When a child discloses information that needs to be passed on to school officials. (This might include personal or family issues indicating a need for ongoing counseling or a disclosure of other serious, nonsexual-abuse-related problems.)

2. When a report needs to be made to the proper authorities, following a child's disclosure of sexual or physical abuse.

Active/Reflective Listening

The key to Private Time is respect for the child, based on our belief that children don't lie about sexual abuse. Whether a child has an abusive experience to relate, has something to say but isn't quite ready to say it, or just wants to make a person-to-person connection with you, a feeling of "What you're telling me is important and I believe you" needs to be conveyed to each child who participates in Private Time.

One way to do this is to employ a basic method of counseling called "active" or "reflective" listening. By restating and reflecting back to the child the essence of what she just told you, you show that you truly heard and understood what the child said. It's important to use your own words, while keeping intact the meaning of what the child said. Otherwise, you may mislead the child or substitute your own interpretation for the child's meaning. Reflective listening requires more than a passive response from the listener. A simple "Uh huh" or "I see" response to a child's statement is not enough.

Actively reflecting the child's meaning is usually done in the form of a question, containing both a "feeling" adjective and the content you just heard. Asking a question gives the child a chance to affirm or negate the reflection. Thus, if a reflection doesn't fit what the child said, he or she can always say, "No, I feel (sad), not (scared)." Here's an example of reflective listening skills used in Private Time:

> **CHILD:** I just don't understand why people do that to kids. I think it's crummy!
>
> **PRESENTER:** You feel kind of confused and angry that people sexually abuse children?
>
> **CHILD:** Yeah. Why are some people so mean?

You can tell that your reflective listening skills are working if the child clarifies or modifies what you just reflected, expands on it, or moves deeper into disclosure. You may need to try a different approach if the child becomes more shy or withdrawn. You can remedy this by saying, "Maybe I didn't understand what you were trying to tell me. Can you tell me again?" **Reflecting back the child's own "feeling" word can be helpful.** If a child doesn't indicate his or her feelings, you can ask an open-ended question ("How did you feel when that happened?"). It's also important to pace your questions and reflections, giving the child ample opportunity to talk.

Due to our desire to find out exactly what has happened to a child, we may feel the need to ask question after question, without pausing to praise the child's efforts, to let her know how brave she is, or to tell her that the abuse is not her fault. It is essential to intersperse your questions with appropriate supportive statements. In addition, asking the child if she has any questions for you can be another way to convey that you truly want to hear what she has to say. When listening to the child's account of the abuse, it is important to phrase your responses in a calm and sensitive manner. Though we may feel horrified by a child's disclosure, we need to put our own feelings aside to make it safe and comfortable for the child to disclose.

Finally, we must be very careful to avoid asking leading questions.

A child usually comes to Private Time with questions or incidents he or she wishes to share. Private Time can also be used as time to brainstorm with a child on an individual basis (e.g., "What would you do if someone touched you in your private parts in a way you didn't like?"). In addition, Private Time offers an opportunity for further education about sexual abuse. For example, the child who comes with concerns about "stranger danger" might be told that usually sexual abuse is usually done by someone known to the child and is not violent. This child might then be asked what she would do to keep safe if someone she knew forced or tricked her into a "no" touch.

Typical Private Time Questions/Responses

A typical Private Time session lasts anywhere from 3 to 10 minutes. Though you'll be using some basic counseling skills with the children, it is important to remember that Private Time is not a 50-minute therapy session. The purpose of Private Time is to

- give children information,

- encourage them to brainstorm their own solutions,

- and determine if a child is currently (or has been in the past) a victim of abuse.

The majority of children come to Private Time for clarification of the material covered during the presentation, to relate the information they've just learned to their own experience, or simply to make a connection with an unfamiliar and exciting visitor.

Many children present "what if" scenarios: "What if someone jumps out of the bushes, grabs you, and puts his hand over your mouth so you can't scream?" The most effective approach to a "what if" is a mixture of instruction and brainstorming. When you turn a question back to the child, coming up with his or her own solutions can be an empowering experience. Encourage children to think of all the resources available to them, such as using funny feelings to keep safe, going into a store to ask for help, running real fast (something kids do better than many adults), and walking home with friends. It's also important to reemphasize that sometimes kids can't stop what's happening. Sometimes even adults can't do this. However, there's always something a child can do afterward: tell someone he or she trusts. Brainstorm with the child about people she or he might tell in this situation. Then proceed to discuss forced or tricked touch by someone known to the child. As mentioned before, children need to be reminded that sexual abuse usually isn't done by a stranger, in the dark, in the park, but rather by someone known to and trusted by the child.

Some children may wish to relate an experience they've had in which they used a funny feeling to keep safe. Others may want to relate incidents they've heard about or seen on TV. Some children may ask hard-to-answer questions, such as, "Why do people do that?" It's usually best to tell the child: "We're not really sure. But it may have something to do with people needing to feel bigger and better about themselves by forcing or tricking younger and smaller people into touch. What we do know is that kids can do a lot of things to keep safe. What could you do if someone forced or tricked you into touching your private parts or theirs?"

Some kids simply want to be your friend, to sing "The Touching Song," or to tell you they like your earrings! By the time some children get to Private Time, they may have forgotten what they wanted to share. This may be another way to put off "telling," but it's important to respect children's own timetables by letting them know that if they remember, they can come back or call at a later date (remind them about the resource card). It's reassuring for the child if you say that sometimes it's hard to talk about some things and you're available if and when she would like to share. In each of the scenarios above, a portion of the time should be used for brainstorming. Before the child leaves, it is also important to ask him if anyone has ever forced or tricked him into touch. Many times, children are just waiting for someone to ask that direct question.

One last comment on "what ifs": when a child's "what ifs" won't go away, even after brainstorming solutions that he or she might use to keep safe, you may be dealing with a child who's feeling vulnerable. He or she may be posing "what if" situations to mask a real one: an abusive situation that he or she can't stop. This is a "red flag" and necessitates further probing.

The next section will cover how to proceed when a child has something to relate that requires a report.

When a Child Discloses Sexual Abuse

Statistics reveal that many children in our society have experienced some form of sexual abuse. During Private Time, children come forward to share frightening details of obscene phone calls they've received; flashers who have exposed themselves to them in parks, museums, or stores; and strangers who have approached them with bribes in exchange for touches. It is important for the presenter to determine when and where each incident occurred and whether an adult has been notified, and to pass on this information to the teacher, school administrator, and parents. It is also essential to support any effort the child made to keep safe, to reflect back the scariness of the incident, and to stress the importance of telling a trusted adult. Children who have had experiences of this type should be told about the reality that kids are usually sexually abused by someone they know, and they should be asked what they would do to keep safe if someone they know and trust abused them.

Children who relate many stories of "stranger danger" may be testing the waters to find out if you can be trusted with something even more scary—an unwanted touch from someone they know. Thus, it is always important to ask if anyone else has ever tried to touch them in their private parts in a way they didn't like. A child who is battling with his or her internal voice, "to tell or not to tell," may fidget or evade eye contact, or try to change the subject. It can be helpful at this time to identify the child's process and stress your willingness to help if he will let you. For example, a presenter might say: "You seem uncomfortable with that question. If someone you know is forcing or tricking you into touch, it can be really hard to tell. If you'd like to tell me, I'd like to help. I'm here to help you keep safe."

It is also important to respect a child's own timetable in telling. There may be great pressure on the child to keep the secret. You may have a strong feeling that this child has experienced inappropriate touch, but, for a myriad of reasons, he or she may find it difficult to disclose the abuse at this time. You might end the Private Time encounter by saying: "I talk with a lot of kids who feel confused about telling. I have a feeling there's something you'd like to tell me, but you're afraid to do so. Why don't you think about it overnight? It's real important to tell to get the touching to stop, and sometimes kids need the help of an adult to do this. You can always call me at this number if you'd like to talk some more. You can also call these other numbers (Children's Protective Services, Counseling Center for Sexually Abused Children, or local Child Abuse Council) if you want to tell someone else about what's troubling you." Giving children the space and per-

mission to tell at their own pace can often have the most beneficial results.

Some children are able to talk about an incident immediately following the presentation. In fact, some kids have been known to disclose during the presentation itself! The children who are ready to disclose the details of their abusive experiences generally fall into two categories:

1. The "I'm telling you, and only you, so please don't tell anyone else" child

2. The "I'm ready to tell to get this touching to stop" child

For your own peace of mind, it is important for you, as the connecting link between the child and the reporting system, to realize that both of these children want the touching to stop. The second child is simply further along in the process of choosing self-protection over protection of the abuser. With the first type of child, it is important to realize that the facts of the abuse and the child's feelings and fears may not be aligned. However, the child's feelings are not the determining factor in making (or not making) a report. "Reasonable Suspicion" on your part means that you have reason to believe, due to the child's testimony, that this child is being or has been sexually abused. Refusing to make a report on the basis of a child's feelings is, in effect, colluding with the offender to maintain the secret. Protection of the child is the bottom line.

How to Elicit Disclosure

There are sensitive, supportive, and caring ways that a presenter can aid a child's disclosure during Private Time. First of all, it is important to compliment the child for telling: "You're doing such a good job! What a brave kid you are! Thank you for sharing this with me. I know how hard it must be to tell." It's also essential to reinforce that no matter what happened, it wasn't the child's fault. Support any efforts the child made to protect her or himself.

Next, it's important to clarify the details of the incident. A child may start by saying, "Something like that happened to me once." The presenter might then ask: "Can you tell me what happened? Did someone force or trick you into touching your private parts or their private parts?"

Other Questions to Ask

- Who touched you? (Try to get names.)

- When did it happen? (Children's sense of time is often different from adults'. Using holidays, birthdays, school days, or weekends can help to pinpoint when the abuse took place.)

- Did it happen more than once?

- Is it still happening?

- Where did she or he touch you? (both the physical location—bedroom, school, at camp, etc.—and where on the body)

- What part of his or her body did he or she use to touch you?

- Did she or he touch you over your clothes or under your clothes?

- Did the abuser ask you to touch him or her over or under the clothes?

- Can you show me/point to where you were touched?

- What do you call that? (use their words)

- Did he touch anyone else? (siblings, friends)

- Did he or she tell you not to tell?

- What else did the abuser say? What did you say?

- Did you tell anyone?

- What made it hard to tell? (determination of threat/risk to child)

- Has anything like this ever happened to you before? Or since?

- Can you tell me about it?

All of these questions should be interspersed with reflections back to the child of both the content of what they've said and the feelings they've expressed, as well as continual encouragement of the child for taking the risk to tell. These are the kinds of questions a social worker and/or police inspector will want included on the Child Abuse Reporting Form. The more information and detail you can provide, the more credible the report will be. However, it is the job of your local Emergency Response Team (such as CPS or the Juvenile Bureau of the Police Department) to do the full investigation.

It is also important to prepare the child as much as possible for what will happen now that she or he has told you, without making false promises to the child. A presenter can tell the child: I'm really glad you trusted me enough to tell me about what happened to you. In order to get this touching to stop, and (if appropriate) to get some help for the offender, I'm going to need to tell someone else. A social worker or police officer may come to school or your house to talk to you and ask you many of the questions I just asked you. If I can be with you, and you'd like me to, I'll try to be there. Can you tell this person just what you told me? Remember what a great job you're doing by telling. You're helping to keep not only yourself safe, but also maybe other kids as well."

Physical Abuse

During Private Time children also may disclose incidents of physical abuse, or incidents involving nonaccidental injury. The physically abused child may tell you that he is getting "no" touches, or may tell you that she gets hit all the time. To distinguish between spanking, or discipline that is nonabusive, and physical abuse, the following questions may be helpful:

- What kind of "no" touches do you get? Can you tell me more about them?

- Do these touches leave marks or bruises on your body?

- Where (on your body) do you get these touches?

- How often do you get hit or touched in this way?

- Who touches you like that?

- What do you get hit with?

- Does the person use objects besides her hand to hit you? What does the person use?

- Does the person tell you not to tell anyone?

- Have you ever told anyone?

As with questions about sexual abuse, it is important to intersperse your questions with reflections of the feeling and content of the child's answers.

The Retracting Child

Sometimes a child may be very open in his or her disclosure—until he or she learns that you'll have to tell someone else. Children's own denial, fear of the consequences, and need to protect the offender often cause them to retract their disclosures. Here are some common forms a retraction might take, along with some effective responses a presenter might use:

CRYING CHILD: *Please don't tell!*

PRESENTER:

1. Support the child's feelings: *I realize how upset you are.*

2. Praise the child for telling: *What a good job you're doing by telling, even though it's hard to.*

3. Inform the child of your role: *My job is to keep kids safe. I'm going to need to tell, to keep you safe and to make sure it doesn't happen again.*

4. Appeal to the part of the child that wants the touching to stop: *The most important thing is for the touch to stop. The only way to be sure it will stop is to tell.*

PROTECTIVE CHILD: My dad loves me. I don't mind. He's not hurting me.

PRESENTER:

1. Support the child's feelings: *Sometimes you can really love the person, and that makes it hard to tell.*

2. Ask for the facts in a sensitive manner:

    Where is Dad touching you?

    When was the last time?

    Does anyone else touch you?

    Does Mom know?

    Do you touch Dad?

    What does Dad say?

What do you say?

Is it a secret?

3. Praise the child for telling: *I'm really glad you're telling me this. You're doing a real good job!*

4. Inform the child of your role: *Even though you may not want me to, I'm going to have to tell someone else.*

5. Appeal to the part of the child that wants the touching to stop: *The most important thing is for the touch to stop, and to keep you safe.*

FRIGHTENED CHILD: *I made it up. Dreamed it. It only happened once.*

PRESENTER:

1. Support the scariness of telling.

2. Ask the child: *What are you afraid might happen if you tell?*

3. Reinforce universality: *I talk to many children who have been sexually abused.*

Many kids are scared to tell because they think they might get in trouble, or they think no one will believe them if they tell. Many children tell me about being forced or tricked into touch, and then get frightened and take it back.

4. Reinforce that you believe: *I really believe you and believe that it happened.*

5. Explain your role: *My job is to help you keep safe. I'm going to need to tell.*

6. Support the part of the child that wants the touch to stop: *I think there's a part of you that wants to get that touch to stop. Sometimes it's hard to do that by yourself. If you tell someone, you can help to keep yourself, and other kids, safe from forced or tricked touch.*

REPORTING PROCEDURE/ DETERMINATION OF RISK

There are three levels of risk that determine the expediency of a report.

Low-Level Risk

Low-level risk to the child is when

● an incident of sexual or physical abuse occurred long ago, in the past,

● the abuser no longer has access to the child (through change in geographical location, death, prison),

● the incident occurred once and didn't involve touching (an obscene phone call or flashing), or

● the case has already been reported and/or prosecuted.

In each of these cases, a report should be made to school administrators and parents. If a child is no longer in danger, yet still traumatized by the event, a counseling referral is in order. Children who have been sexually abused tend to minimize the abuse. Thus, cases that appear to be of low-level risk should be checked out carefully. A written child abuse report should be filed to prevent the abuse of other children, even if there is no longer danger to this particular child.

Medium-Level Risk

Medium-Level Risk to the child involves cases in which the abuse is recent or current, but the abuser does not live with the child, and the child is not in immediate danger of re-abuse.

In these cases, a phone call must be made (within 24 hours) to Children's Protective Services or the proper reporting agency in your community. In California, a written child abuse reporting form must be filed within 36 hours of the child's disclosure. The actual Child Abuse Reporting Form varies from state to state, so you should contact your state Department of Social Services or Justice Department for this form. For further information on what needs to be reported and to whom, see the section "Reporting Information for Teachers" on page 55. If the abuser is not related to the child, parents may be notified, and the family should be referred to counseling.

High-Level Risk

High-Level Risk to the child occurs when the abuser lives in the home or has daily access to the child, and the probability of re-abuse in the immediate future is very high.

In these cases a call to the local reporting agency should be made immediately and a written report should be filed within 36 hours. Arrangements should be made that day to take the child into a shelter (police officers are authorized to do this) to prevent re-abuse from happening. If the last incident of sexual abuse happened within 24 hours, a child might be taken to the local Child Abuse Victim Services agency for a medical exam, prior to being taken to the shelter. If the abuser is a family member, the child's family should not be informed of the abuse by the presenter. The investigative unit will do this.

It is important to function as a team, with one person designated as the team leader. In most cases in which reports must be made, it is helpful to designate one prevention worker as the link between the child and the child abuse reporting system. If this is your arrangement, presenters should be asked to inform the team leader when they feel a report needs to be made. The team leader would then carry out the above steps.

How to Deal with Personal Feelings

Private Time can be an exhilarating experience for presenters, knowing that they may be the first person a child has told about a previously taboo subject, and that they can now act as the first link to getting help for the child. However, Private Time can be a traumatic and emotional experience for the presenter as well. At times our own denial can affect our listening ability. Perhaps a certain child reminds us of the way we used to look when we were young. We may also find it difficult to believe that someone would actually do such a thing to a child. Or we may not be able to believe that a mother, grandfather, or day-care worker could really commit such a crime. Our own denial may cause us to minimize what the child is saying, to overreact to the child's disclosure, or to otherwise distract the child from telling. In order to be effective prevention specialists, it is important to recognize these feelings within us all, verbalize them to supportive copresenters, and to begin to let go of our own denial.

Our personal feelings can also surface in other ways. We may leave a Private Time session feeling we haven't done enough or said the right thing: "If only I'd said 'such and such' he would have trusted me enough to tell me what happened." It is of the utmost importance at these times to realize that we offer an invaluable service through our presentations and the model we provide during Private Time: that of respecting, listening to, and believing children.

Our primary focus is prevention: *Giving children the permission and language to prevent unwanted touches. If we give one child the message that it's okay to tell, that we believe her or him, and that we're available when he or she is ready to tell, we've already done a tremendous job!*

School Follow-Up

1. Structured or unstructured follow-up to *Keeping Kids Safe* presentations at schools can be very beneficial and reinforcing for the children.

2. Presenters will need to decide how much, if any, follow-up they will do at each school they serve.

3. Issues of staff time, possible reports, and scheduling all need to be addressed.

4. The type of relationship you have with a school and its staff will determine whether or not follow-up services are offered.

FOLLOW-UP OPTIONS

One option is to show a video following the school workshops. It is preferable to return to a school after all the classroom presentations have been completed to show a video (age appropriate) in an auditorium setting to the upper and lower grades. This gives children another opportunity to review the material, to speak to someone, to ask questions that have arisen since our last presentation to their class, or to disclose abuse.

Another option is to return to a school, unscheduled, to speak to specific "red flag" children. It's a good idea to make yourself available for several hours, so that as many children as possible see you and therefore have the opportunity to approach you if they choose.

Finally, you may want to schedule a follow-up meeting with the principal and staff to discuss outcomes, issues, reports. Include time to "hang out" before school, at lunch or recess, or after school to interact with children, giving them the opportunity to approach you.

Combating Denial

THE PREVENTION WORKER AND DENIAL

One of the most pervasive roadblocks to the successful prevention of or early intervention in a child sexual abuse is denial, the defense mechanism used in varying degrees by most of us when we are confronted with the horror of child sexual abuse. We simply don't want to know of its existence. Even those of us who work in the fields and know how prevalent child sexual abuse is, may sometimes be faced with our own denial.

Denial manifests itself in many subtle and not-so-subtle ways:

1. Not believing children

2. Discrediting children's ability to tell the truth

3. Discrediting experts when they support children

4. Minimizing: "It only happened once," "it wasn't full intercourse," etc.

5. Blaming the child: "She asked for it by wearing sexy clothes."

6. Not hearing "clues" children drop—or even clear statements about the abuse— e.g., "He touched me here," pointing to genitals, and we say, "Oh, you mean your tummy."

7. Believing myths, e.g., the "dangerous stranger"; not being open to facts

Since presenters' denial is a factor in working with children during *Keeping Kids Safe* workshops and Private Time, it is important that we get in touch with our feelings regarding abuse. The following exercise may help.

Denial Exercise

Close your eyes. Imagine the person (adult) who is closest to you, and who you trust implicitly. Hold the picture (image) of that person in your mind. Now, imagine that you just received the news that this person recently molested a 5-year-old.

1. What was your immediate reaction? How did you feel?

2. What did you do or feel next?

Discussion

Many people who do this exercise are surprised to find that they could not believe someone they knew and trusted was capable of abusing a child. How did you react? If you found yourself changing the image of the person to a stranger or someone less close to you, that's your denial showing. Did you believe the news? Many people who do this exercise attempt to discredit the bearer of the news. How did you handle it?

Finally, if you reached a point where you believed and accepted the abuse as a reality, you achieved the goal of this exercise. To work effectively toward the prevention and early detection of child sexual abuse we must believe that anyone (even our most beloved) is capable of abusing children.

Denial—How It Looks in the World

The defense mechanism of denial is not limited to the prevention worker who—in denial about the possibility of abuse—minimizes, distorts, or exaggerates a child's disclosure during Private Time. Research shows that denial of both the existence and seriousness of child sexual abuse is pervasive in our society—within individuals, adults, and children alike; within school systems; and even within child abuse response systems themselves. As prevention workers, we encounter denial in every aspect of our work.

In attempting to set up and carry out *Keeping Kids Safe* workshops at a school, a prevention worker may come across denial in the following scenarios:

Denial in the School System

The principal, director, or coordinator

- may never quite be able to make all the arrangements necessary to have the *Keeping Kids Safe* program come to the school

- may say that the parents are not interested; sexual abuse doesn't happen in their neighborhood; or the school population is culturally "different" and therefore unable to make use of prevention information

- may say that their calendar is filled for the year, with art projects, field trips, etc.

- may say that teachers are too busy to fit the *Keeping Kids Safe* program into their schedule, that not all teachers want *Keeping Kids Safe* Workshops in their classrooms, or that they can't seem to find a free afternoon for a teacher's meeting

- may give erroneous or confusing information to teachers concerning presentations, or may forget that something else was scheduled for that day and cancel the *Keeping Kids Safe* workshop

- may be extremely inflexible in scheduling the children's workshop and Private Time; may say lunch can't be changed, recess can't be changed, teachers' breaks can't be changed

- may interrupt *Keeping Kids Safe* classes with phone calls, loudspeaker announcements, or emergency drills

- may not want to know anything about a report, may try to block a report from being made, may insist that they know the family and that it is incapable of abuse, or say that the child in question is a troublemaker

Teachers/Aides/School Personnel

- may say that the *Keeping Kids Safe* program will scare the children, or that the children are not old enough to understand the material

- may say they've already talked to the children about sexuality, sex education, or molestation; that the program is good in general, but not needed in their class

- may be inflexible in terms of changing schedules (recess, lunch, lesson plan) or changing the room environment (moving chairs and desks to accommodate a semicircle)

- may "forget" that the *Keeping Kids Safe* program was scheduled to come to their class, may have scheduled a field trip on the day of presentation, or may not want to make time in their schedule for the 2-day presentation

- may continuously interrupt the children's workshop, may not stay in the classroom during the presentation, or may be there "in body only," using the presentation time to grade papers

- may tell children that they don't have to go to Private Time or that they don't have to go the second day; may rush children off to lunch or recess after the presentation, discouraging Private Time participation by their actions, if not their words

- may fall asleep or continually talk to other faculty during the staff workshop

- may harshly discipline or remove children during the children's workshop

- may discredit children's disclosures ("that child has an active imagination," "always lies," or "comes from a lovely family.")

Denial from Parents

Parent denial may surface during parent meetings. Parents are often concerned that the prevention information may scare their children, may be over their heads, or may turn them off to touches of all kinds, from hugs to baths to spankings. Some parents want to discuss this sensitive issue with their children in their own way and do not want *Keeping Kids Safe* to cover it in the classroom setting.

When approached by prevention workers or school personnel about an incident of abuse their child has experienced, parents may show their denial in the following ways:

- They may insist that their child has an active imagination, needs a lot of attention, or was never left alone with the accused offender.

- They may feel hurt or angry that their child didn't tell them right away or disclosed the incident to a stranger.

- They may not believe or may discredit their child, especially if they denied abuse in their own past.

Denial from Children

Children often demonstrate their denial in two situations:

1. during the classroom presentation

2. during the Private Time encounter

In class a child:

- may be angry or very disruptive during the workshop

- may fall asleep (during the incest sequence, perhaps)

- may be shy, quiet, or withdrawn during the children's presentation (the kind of child who seems to be invisible)

- may look sad or depressed (especially during Uncle Sam or Incest skits)

- may ask a lot of questions or raise his or her hand to be called on and forget the question when recognized

During Private Time, children who are in denial tend to retract the disclosure they made the previous day. They may say, "It was only a dream," "I made it up," or "I don't remember what I said or who touched me." Or they may say, "He only did it once. I know he won't do it anymore." They may insist that "It is *too* the child's fault." They may say there is no one they can talk to or trust, and nothing they can do to keep safe from unwanted touches. Children who are identified by the presenters or observer as "red flags" during the workshop may not want to come to Private Time when asked to do so. If they participate in Private Time, they may insist that everything is fine and they have never been forced or tricked into touch, even though the *Keeping Kids Safe* worker suspects otherwise. Children who won't give up the "Super Hero" image, even when they're repeatedly encouraged to think of ways to keep safe by using their brains, may also demonstrate denial (e.g., "I'd karate chop him if he got near me"). They are refusing to acknowledge what they'd really do if they encountered an abusive touch.

Denial from the System

Denial is also prevalent in the child abuse reporting system itself. Social workers and criminal justice personnel may show their denial:

- by continually maintaining that the reports from *Keeping Kids Safe* prevention educators are unfounded or are annoying additions to their workload

- by viewing the efforts of prevention programs as overzealous and unnecessary

- by characterizing fondling or initially abusive touches to children as unimportant or unworthy of follow-up

As you can see, denial runs rampant in our society, from the workers who don't want to hear one more report; to the principal who knows the family; to the parent who rationalizes the child's distress; to the response system that's overworked, overloaded, and suspicious of prevention projects. The more credible the accused offender, the less credible the child becomes. It's essential to counteract denial in our work, to continue to maintain that "the emperor has no clothes" even when everyone around us says, "He does!"

3

Classroom Management

Helpful Hints for Classroom Management

The following hints for working with children in the classroom have proven helpful to presenters.

PARTICIPATION

If children are not participating, try the following:

- **Move around** from one side of the room to the other, turn your back on the class momentarily, then turn around quickly and ask a question or give information.

- **Use children's names** in the presentation (e.g., "What if Cheryl was walking down the street and…").

- If asking questions and getting no response, **give part of the answer** as a lead-in. (For instance, you might ask "What are your three special body rights? The right to say…" then let the children finish the sentence.)

- If a child volunteers to do a role-play and then "freezes up," one of the presenters can **whisper suggestions in the child's ear** and let the child repeat.

TALKING

If children are talking, try the following:

- **Use the name of a child talking in the presentation** or in your next sentence; e.g., "and one of your special body rights, Johnny, is...".

- **Direct the next question also to a child who is talking.**

RESTLESSNESS

If the children are getting restless, do the following:

- Try **standing up for a stretch** when it's appropriate.

- **Take only one answer** to each question and then move on to the next question.

- Try **stopping all action** (perhaps both presenters sit down). When the class quiets down, address the children's embarrassment and the importance of the topic. Only continue when the class is ready (sitting quietly).

- If the restlessness is due to the children's being unable to hear other children's responses to questions, **try repeating each child's answer** as you go on to the next child.

- If the children are forgetting to raise their hands or are being disruptive, presenters can **give positive reinforcement** by saying, "Joseph has his hand up" and calling on Joseph to answer the question.

- If a child is playing with his or her name tag or some other object and is being disruptive, the observer or presenter can **walk over to the child, take the object** and tell him or her that **he or she can have it back after the presentation.**

IN GENERAL

It is important for presenters to **pay attention to the total group**—not just the child who is talking. A **light touch** on the back of the head can **remind a distracted child to wait** for a turn to talk.

Additional Suggestions

- **If a child has the appropriate answer to a question, emphasize it** by repeating it to the class.

- **Use the words of the children;** don't change them. You can add to or expand on the children's statements by adding "maybe" or "perhaps." For example:

  CHILD: Gay people abuse children.

  PRESENTER: Maybe some gay people abuse children. Can people who aren't gay abuse children?... Sure. Most of the time it's straight people who force or trick children into touch.

  It is empowering for the child to have her or his own perceptions validated.

- Addressing the "Super Hero/Karate Champ/Tuff Guy" Syndrome:

  Correct myths—most of the time the abuser is not a stranger. Most of the time it's a person the child knows, a person who is nice to children.

  Talk about the size difference between a child and an adult offender. Say, "Most children won't hit someone much bigger than they are; most of the time children won't hit an uncle or a dad."

- If a child responds to the Tickle or Bully role-play by saying, "I'd hit him," say, "What happens when you hit someone? They hit you back. Then you could have a fight and end up in more trouble or possibly even get hurt." Then ask the child, "What could you really do, using your brain?"

  Validate that it is okay for the child to hit or kick someone if it gives the child time to get away and be safe. Keeping safe is different from beating up the other person.

Role of the Observer

The observer is a helpful but *optional* part of the classroom presentation team. Overall, the observer's role is to facilitate the presentation, reduce distractions, and note children's behavior and statements. However, staffing considerations may make it impossible to have a working team of three presenters. In this case, the curriculum can be adapted for two presenters.

When Available, the Observer Is Responsible for the Following:

- Complete the Observer/Presentation Form each day and place it in the portfolio at the end of each class

- Help arrange the room, if necessary, and put name tags on the children

- Lead the applause after each role-play when a child has volunteered

- Make a note of "red flag" behaviors or statements, along with the child's name, on the Observer/Presentation Form

- Sing "The Touching Song" along with the presenters

- Silently cue the presenters if they need to move posters to be more easily seen, if they need to speak louder, or if there is a child who is anxious to participate but has not been acknowledged

- Note on the Observer/Presentation Form the names of children who sign up for Private Time

- Help to conduct Private Time

Classroom Management Tips for Observers

- If a student is being disruptive, it usually helps to stand behind the child, touch his or her arm or shoulder, and softly remind the child not to talk.

- If two or more children are distracted or disruptive, the observer can sit between them.

- If the children continue to be disruptive, quietly have one of them move to the other side of the room and exchange seats with a quiet child.

- If a child is playing with an item, quietly take it and tell the child you'll return it after the presentation.

- In extreme cases only, if a child is continuously disruptive and refuses to sit quietly, have the child leave the semicircle and sit with you or the teacher outside of the circle. We don't send children out of the room as a rule.

- Position yourself so that you can move from one side of the room to the other unobtrusively, to be able to anticipate minor distractions and prevent them from becoming major disruptions.

- With preschool or kindergarten children, have a child sit on your lap or on the floor between your legs if she or he has difficulty focusing.

Respecting Differences

Working with children from culturally diverse groups or who have physical, mental, learning, or emotional disabilities can be challenging. If you are going to provide services for all children, then you must have a systematic and organized plan that is inclusive of all children and communities. Some suggestions are outlined below.

BEING SENSITIVE TO ECONOMIC AND CULTURAL DIVERSITY

Personal Attitudes

It is important to follow the *Keeping Kids Safe* curriculum in order to avoid spontaneous remarks that might reveal unconscious personal bias or stereotyping of cultural groups. The process will become more natural with practice.

Logistics/Scheduling

Make sure presentations are made available to schools attended by low-income and ethnic minority children. Fees may be reduced if it seems appropriate to do so.

Staffing

Use ethnically diverse staff and volunteers to make linkages. Work with staff from the community and with other community representatives to make sure materials (songs, handouts, curricula, etc.) are appropriately translated into all necessary languages.

Role-Modeling Respectful Relationships

Since most presentations are made by two people, care should be taken to make sure that the person representing the dominant culture doesn't make all the decisions; decisions should be made equally. For example, in a male/female pairing, the male is sometimes the victim; the female the offender. If there is a difference of opinion, it's a good idea to expose a problem-solving process and to not automatically assume that the white person's opinion counts more than the nonwhite person's.

Staff/Parent Presentations

Be aware of the customs, language, and specific concerns of different cultures. For example, you may need to conduct parent meetings in different languages simultaneously. Your local school district may provide translators or translate handouts.

Newly Arrived Children

Special attention should be paid to children who have recently arrived in the United States. Often there are differences in both language and customs. Especially when children come from non-Western cultures, culture shock should be expected. It is important that presenters pay attention to cues from the children regarding possible differences. For example, children from a different culture may not be as accustomed as native-born American children to talking about things that happen inside the family. This difference should be respected.

Translated Presentations

When necessary, the curriculum may be translated simultaneously by a bilingual teacher, aide, or presenter, to ensure that monolingual children receive the information in their own language.

Child Advocacy

If you need to make a report of sexual abuse and the child must be connected with the criminal justice system, you should be prepared to

- translate for a monolingual child,

- use American Sign Language for a child with a hearing impairment, and

- advocate for all children. This is especially important for ethnic minority, low-income, or disabled children, who are particularly vulnerable because of stereotyping and system denial.[2]

Self-Esteem Building

Presentation of the *Keeping Kids Safe* curriculum helps children build a positive self-image by:

- **recognizing that all children can contribute.** Presenters need to call on all children and must be conscious of their own possible preconceptions regarding who might know the right answers.

- **reducing ethnic, class, and disability stereotypes.** The curriculum's posters show that that all kinds of people can sexually abuse children and that it happens to all kinds of children.

- **empowering all children with information.** Information concerning children's body rights and their right to say "no" to unwanted touches is provided.

- **using names and examples in skits relevant to the culture(s) of the children.** For instance, ministers are cited as resources in the Black community; older siblings as resources in large families.

WORKING WITH CHILDREN WHO HAVE PHYSICAL, MENTAL, LEARNING, OR EMOTIONAL DISABILITIES

Personal Attitudes

First and foremost, if you've never had the experience, you must examine your own feelings about working with children with disabilities. You need to decide what special training you need to arrange for your staff.

Logistics/Scheduling

You need to decide how special education classes will be incorporated into your regular presentation schedule.

Outreach/Staffing

When appropriate, hire staff who represent the disabled populations in the community.

---

[2] An in-depth discussion of the vulnerabilities of children with disabilities, and prevention strategies that address these vulnerabilities, may be found in the manual, *I'm Somebody— A Child Sexual Abuse Prevention Manual for Children with Disabilities,* by Pnina Tobin, Cathe Carpenter, and Laura Rifkin (1996). Available through PMT Consultants.

4

Working with Parents, Teachers, and the Schools

SCHEDULING *KEEPING KIDS SAFE* WORKSHOPS

To schedule presentations, the following general procedures should be observed:

1. Arrangements regarding date, time, and room number must be made with school personnel for staff workshops, parent workshops, and classroom presentation(s).

2. Make sure that the school administrator (principal, director, site manager, head teacher, etc.) is aware of the arrangements.

3. The staff workshop should precede the parent workshop. This prepares teachers to answer questions that parents might have and also enables teachers to encourage parent attendance at the parent workshop.

4. The parent workshop, often scheduled at night to accommodate working parents, should be scheduled at least one week before the classroom presentations begin. This allows time for parents to receive and return permission slips. Permission slips should be sent out to all parents, in appropriate languages, whether they attended the parent workshop or not.

5. Classroom presentations should be scheduled taking into account lunchtime, recess, holidays, staff availability, and other special school programs. Private Time should be arranged with the principal when classroom presentations are scheduled. This will allow for smooth handling of this delicate portion of the program.

Introduction to Staff and Parent Meetings

Before making our presentations to children, we always conduct two meetings: one for school staff and one school-wide meeting for parents. Parents and teachers care for children and are vitally concerned about protecting them from sexual abuse. At the same time, this is a sensitive issue. **Parents have the right to make final decisions about their child's participation.**

Staff and parents are looking for:

- information on the issue of child sexual abuse,

- guidance on how to recognize it,

- advice on what can be done to protect their children, and

- a forum in which to voice their concerns and have their questions answered.

Staff and parent meetings are essential because of the pivotal role of these caretaking adults in the children's lives. While we are with a class of children for an hour or less per day, for 2 days, their parents and teachers are with them daily. We must have the permission and support of these significant adults to ensure that our prevention message is reinforced. Though parents and teachers are genuinely concerned about child sexual abuse, there is confusion as to how to talk about it and what to do about it.

The staff and parent meetings should be conducted in a relaxed atmosphere. It is the time for staff or parents to take in new and sensitive information, ask questions, and express their concerns. Our responses must be respectful, consistent, honest, and concrete.

GOALS FOR STAFF MEETINGS AND PARENT MEETINGS

Participants give:

- their permission for us to present the workshop to the children

- support for key concepts of the curriculum

- their willingness to reinforce the prevention message with children and other adults

Participants leave the meeting with the following information:

- The best protection is to prepare a child to help himself or herself.

- Child sexual abuse can happen to anyone, and if it happens it isn't the child's fault.

- "Do"s and "don't"s for when a child discloses abuse.

Participants leave the meeting with the following skills:

- A knowledge of the common indicators of child sexual abuse—what to look for

- A common language to talk about sexual abuse

- The ability to talk with (empower) children in regard to sexual abuse

- The ability to listen to (believe) children about sexual abuse

Parents and teachers are their children's best resource.

PARENT AND STAFF MEETINGS HAVE TWO COMPONENTS

1. The meetings are informative and orderly, providing brief explanations of child sexual abuse, telling why children need self-protection, and giving a summary of our philosophy and methods.

2. The meetings respond to the questions and concerns of parents and staff.

Note: *The following sections will outline how to present staff and parent meetings, respectively.*

Staff Meetings

LOGISTICS

The dates, times, and places for staff meetings are usually scheduled with the principal, director, or head teacher. The staff meeting is held prior to the parent meeting (which is held, if possible, 1 week before the children's workshop), usually during school hours, at a regular staff meeting time. Up to 1 hour should be allowed for the meeting. Afterwards, teachers are able to encourage parents to attend the parent meeting and answer their questions.

Both the program staff and the school personnel have a responsibility for preparing for the staff meeting. The following breakdown of tasks is typical.

School Administrator's Responsibilities

1. Notify staff of the meeting date and time and require their attendance

2. Secure a room for the meeting

3. Provide refreshments, if any

4. Introduce *Keeping Kids Safe* presenters to staff at the beginning of the meeting

Program Staff's Responsibilities

1. Determine the number of staff who will participate in the meeting and the number of handouts needed

2. Know the location of the meeting

3. Schedule two *Keeping Kids Safe* presenters to conduct the meeting

4. Bring a sufficient number of handouts

5. Bring a portfolio (with posters and touch signs), books, and puppets

6. Have the presenters divide responsibility for sections of the presentation

7. Conduct the meeting

Materials Needed for Staff Meeting

1. Handouts (translated where appropriate)

2. Reporting law

3. Permission slips

4. Follow-up activities list

5. Tapes of "The Touching Song" for sale

6. Books for sale (when available)

Presentation and Stage Directions

MEETING PREPARATION

1. Place handout materials in an accessible place.

2. Place two chairs in front of the room for the presenters.

2. Take posters and touch signs out of the portfolio and place them next to the presenters' chairs.

ROOM SETUP

1. Presenters are seated in chairs in front of the room. Project and presenters are introduced by name by the principal (or director, or head teacher).

TEACHER PRESENTATION OUTLINE

Introduction

THANK SCHOOL ADMINISTRATOR FOR INTRODUCTION

OVERVIEW OF WHAT WILL BE COVERED

1. The issue of child sexual abuse (statistics and scope of problem)

2. The effects of abuse

3. Reasons children are vulnerable to abuse

4. Basic *Keeping Kids Safe* concepts

5. A brief overview of the children's program

6. Discussion of resources

7. What teachers can do to protect their children from abuse and to reinforce the program information

8. Question-and-answer period at end of presentation (questions also will be entertained at any other point during the presentation)

Statistics

It is estimated that one in three girls and one in seven boys is sexually abused before the age of 18 (though many experts now think it's closer to one in three girls and one in four boys).

An even more significant statistic is that 75 to 85 percent of the time, the person who abuses the child is not a stranger. Rather, it is someone known to the child—someone in the child's support system—such as a family member, friend of the family, neighbor, or babysitter.

Effects on Kids

Sexual abuse can leave extremely negative long-term effects on a child.

Children who are sexually abused typically feel guilty. They feel that the abuse is their fault, that they caused it, or that they should have stopped it somehow.

Children who have been sexually abused usually feel powerless. Because sexual abuse is primarily an issue of a power imbalance—a bigger, older person taking advantage of a smaller, younger person—children who are being abused often feel they can do nothing to stop the abuse, that they are helpless.

Children who have been sexually abused are burdened with having to live with a shameful secret. One of the typical features of child sexual abuse is that the child is forced or manipulated into keeping the abuse a secret. This is one of the main clues to the child that something is wrong. The fact that the child is coerced or bribed into secrecy about a touch indicates that the touch is not okay. When the child is touched in an acceptable fashion there is no pressure to keep the touch a secret. For example, when a parent tucks a child in at bedtime, there's no instruction to the child to keep the goodnight kiss and hug a secret.

Victims often feel isolated from their peers. They feel that no one understands. They know that they have had experiences that are different from the experiences of other children.

If the sexual abuse is not treated, the sexually abused child may experience long-term effects. Teenage runaway behavior, teen prostitution, drug and alcohol abuse, depression, and suicide have all been linked to abusive experiences in childhood. The perpetrators of child sexual abuse often have a history of having been sexually abused as children. Furthermore, the ability to trust and to form intimate relationships is often adversely affected in survivors of child sexual abuse. When someone close to a child violates the child's boundaries and trust, it is difficult for the child to trust and become intimate in adult relationships.

Why Children Are Vulnerable

Sexual abuse is fundamentally an issue of power imbalance. We're talking about a bigger person, an older person, taking advantage of a younger, smaller person.

Children are totally dependent on adults, both physically and emotionally. Adults may take advantage of this dependency by threatening the withdrawal of physical or emotional support, or by manipulating the child's need for affection. Children are taught blind obedience to adult authority, leaving them vulnerable to those untrustworthy adults who would talk them into sexual abuse.

Adults are more powerful, physically and psychologically, than children. An adult can usually overpower a child. Even though many adults do not use physical force to coerce a

child into sexual abuse, the child's knowledge that the potential exists may be threatening.

Children believe the myth of the "dangerous stranger." Children are taught to avoid being in dark alleys, taking candy from strangers, or getting into a car with an unknown adult. Yet recent research reveals that, over 85 percent of the time, children know and often trust their abuser. He is often a relative or a family friend. Children, therefore, while looking out for strangers who look and act odd or different from them, are unprotected 85 percent of the time.

All children, by virtue of their dependent, second-class status with respect to adults, feel "not good enough." Any adult can easily prey on a child's need to feel unique, valued, and special. Children are vulnerable to these approaches, especially if they are not valued by those closest to them.

Basic Keeping Kids Safe Concepts

We view our presentations not as sex education, but, rather, as personal body safety—kind of like traffic safety. When we're teaching children about crossing the street, we tell them to use the traffic lights, look both ways, and not to play in the street. We don't describe to them what they would feel like or look like if they were hit by a truck. Similarly, when we talk about sexual abuse, we talk about it just like any other personal safety issue. That is, we talk to children about uncomfortable situations they might find themselves in. And we brainstorm with them about how they can protect themselves with skills they already have—like running, yelling, saying "no," calling for help, or telling someone they trust.

We teach children about three kinds of touches.

1. The first touch is a **"heart" touch.** That's a touch that *both* people like and want.

2. Then there is a **"no" touch.** A "no" touch is a touch that you don't like—a touch that does not feel good to you.

3. Finally there is a **"question mark" touch.** A "question mark" touch is a confusing, mixed-up touch.

We tell children that they have special body rights—they have the right to feel safe, to say "no," and to ask questions if somebody tries to touch them in a way that they don't like.

We tell children that no one has a right to force or trick them into touching private parts of their own body or the other person's body.

Highlights of the Keeping Kids Safe Children's Program

Children's workshops are held in two sessions, 30 minutes to an hour each, on 2 consecutive days. Presentations are given by a team of two or three trained staff and/or volunteers.

SESSION 1: On the first day, we define sexual abuse and body safety in language the children can understand. For example, the elementary school curriculum defines sexual abuse as "forced or tricked touch to private parts of your body or the other person's body." We identify the private parts of the body. We also identify three special body rights that all children have: the right to be safe, the right to say "no," and the right to ask questions about touches.

Next, we discuss touches that children like ("heart" touches), and dislike ("no" touches), and those touches that are confusing ("?" touches). Presenters do four to six skits designed to illustrate various kinds of touches. With preschool and early elementary school children, colorful, child-sized puppets are used to illustrate and identify touches. Older elementary school children identify touches themselves by voting.

In keeping with our philosophy of never leaving a child in a vulnerable position, each skit identified as showing a "?" or "no" touch is replayed, using children as actors and getting suggestions from the class. In this way, we always model a positive outcome for the children. Skills suggested by the class and presenters are already in a child's repertoire of behavior; they include running away, saying "no" or "stop," and telling someone the child trusts about the touch (getting help). It is extremely empowering for children to be able to practice prevention skills with their peers in preparation for real-life situations. Since many children blame themselves for the abuse, *we emphasize repeatedly that if a child cannot stop a touch, it is never the child's fault.*

We sing "The Touching Song" with both younger and older children to illustrate the three kinds of touches. We'd like to sing it for you now and do several of our skits to demonstrate our elementary curriculum. We'll start with the Tickle Play and when we're done, we'll ask you to vote on what kind of touch it is. Just act like you are children for a minute. *(Demonstrate the tickle touch. Hold up appropriate touch signs, encouraging teachers to vote. Ask what kind of a touch it was. Then ask what a child could do to keep herself safe. Redo the skit with a positive outcome.)*

Now we're going to show you the Uncle Sam skit. In this skit I'm going to be Uncle Sam. The other presenter will be my niece, Pam, and she's going to be the age of the children in your child's class. We're going to be at a family dinner. Let's see what happens. What kind of touch is this for Pam? *(Demonstrate the Uncle Sam skit. Hold up appropriate touch signs, encouraging teachers to vote. Ask what kind of a touch it was. Then ask what Pam could do to keep herself safe. Redo the skit with a positive outcome. Then sing "The Touching Song.")*

SESSION 2: The concepts presented during Session 1 are reviewed and expanded upon during Session 2. The children are told that sexual abuse can happen anywhere, at any time of the day or night, to any child, rich or poor, black, brown, or white. We also stress that all kinds of people can sexually abuse children. They may be strangers or people the child knows. In this way, we dispel myths children commonly believe about child sexual abuse.

Next, we introduce the concept of intuition or funny feelings, the "inner voice" in each of us that warns us something is about to happen. We believe children can employ this internal warning system as another tool to keep themselves safe. Age-appropriate skills are demonstrated to show children how they can use their funny feelings. Once again, children replay skits using safety suggestions from presenters and the class.

Now we want to show you a portion of our early elementary curriculum that teaches the concept of funny feelings to young children. In this skit Yellow Puppet is a little boy who's 6 years old. Purple Puppet is his babysitter who wants to play a game that gives Johnny a funny feeling. Safety Friend helps Johnny to identify his funny feelings. (*Demonstrate Funny Feeling skit and redo the skit with a positive outcome.*)

Presenters also discuss bribery and give children practice in stranger identification in order to prepare them for possible stranger molestation. Children learn how to do a self-defense yell—a low-pitched, loud yell from deep in the diaphragm—which can be used to warn adults that the child needs help or to scare away the potential molester.

Finally, since children are most often molested by someone they know, we include a sequence on incest. Children are shown an initial approach to a daughter by the father, the reaction of an unbelieving mother, and a scene in which the child is believed and gets help. Children are taught new skills to help them deal with the more subtle manipulation by a caregiver or family member. Children are involved as friends who help the child to tell in the final skit of this sequence. This allows them to practice newly acquired skills and internalize them for future use.

Private Time

At the end of each session, we offer children a chance to ask us questions and clear up confusion about touches. This portion of the program is called "Private Time" and usually takes place in the 30 minutes immediately following the presentation. We are available to interact with the younger children on a one-to-one basis, reviewing what to do to keep safe and who to tell.

Children who have experienced abuse may approach presenters for help at this time. Children may also go to their parents or teachers for help after the presentation. That's why it is important to familiarize yourself with indicators of abuse and available resources. We'll be covering this information in the next portion of our program.

Note to Presenters: *After completing this description of the children's program, we discuss resources, give out the handouts, and make suggestions about what teachers can do after we've made our presentation to the children.*

Resources

Before we take questions from the group, we briefly review resources that are available to teachers. We also discuss what teachers can do, following our classroom presentation, to reinforce the information with their own children.

What Teachers Can Do

During the Staff Meeting. Teachers are key to our presentation. We need the teachers' support in order to make the most effective presentation possible. When teachers show interest and support, children will focus their attention on the content. The teacher's role continues after we have completed our presentation. Teachers can reinforce the main points of our prevention message and can serve as a trusted resource for a child who has been sexually abused.

During the Presentation. It is very important that teachers help in several ways. We need teachers to help us rearrange the room so the children can sit in a semicircle. The teacher is also needed to help us with classroom management, sitting with the children, separating two children who should not sit together, or redirecting the attention of a distracted child toward the presentation. We encourage teachers to sing along with us as they pick up the chorus of the song.

Before and after the Presentation. If there is a child that the teacher has some concerns about regarding sexual abuse, we urge the teacher to indicate his or her concerns before or after our presentation.

Sexual abuse is against the law. **All who work with children are mandated by law to report reasonable suspicion of child abuse.** One of the handouts is a summary of the (California) reporting law. If you have reasonable suspicion that a child is being sexually abused, you must report it.

Some indicators of possible sexual abuse include, but are not limited to: radical change in behavior; repeated seductive behavior toward adults; sudden fear of a person the child formerly liked; compulsive or excessive sex play with other children; compulsive masturbation in class or on the playground; redness or swelling in the genital area. Also watch out for children who seem tired and fall asleep in class, who have adult "friends" or a possessive caregiver, who overdress as if to hide their body, or who seem depressed.

When you have some concerns about a child, and feel that there is something troubling him, include sexual abuse as one of the possible problems. When talking with the child, ask: "Are you upset? Is something bothering you?" Also include: "Is someone touching you in the private parts of your body?"

Reporting Procedure. When a child tells us that someone has touched him or her in private parts of his or her body, giving us specific details, we interpret this as "reasonable suspicion to believe." We then work with the school to report the abuse. We interpret "reasonable suspicion" to mean that a child has reported that somebody is touching him or her in private parts of the child's body. We believe children when they say this to us and we make up a report.

Our process for reporting is that we work with the child to get the details, and then we share the information with the principal and other appropriate people at the school. We contact the reporting agency directly, although every community should set up the specific arrangements for doing this, based on the local situation.

There are several local agencies that provide help for abused children. (Provide local resources at this time.) We also are a resource. If you have a question about something covered in our presentation, we are available to answer it. If you have a question about a child—if you feel something is wrong and you are not sure how to proceed—you also should call: (insert local child abuse reporting agency). We have brought a handout about reporting information for your future use.

Teacher Follow-Up Activities

1. See Appendix C: "Parent and Teacher Follow-Up Exercises"

2. Teachers are encouraged to incorporate books on sexual abuse prevention into their lesson plans. We particularly recommend *No More Secrets,* by Caren Adams and Jennifer Fay, *Come Tell Me Right Away,* by Linda Tschirhart Sanford, and *He Told Me Not To Tell,* by Jennifer Fay. These are well-written texts with a focus on helping adults talk more clearly to kids about sexual abuse. We also suggest *Red Flag Green Flag People* by Joy Williams. This is a coloring book that helps kids to understand the concepts of private parts, touches, and who to tell.

3. Teachers can show appropriate videos on sexual abuse, such as "Strong Kids, Safe Kids."

4. Selected TV programs can be recommended based on age appropriateness.

Concluding Remarks

We will be in your classroom for 2 days. We ask that you set up your room in a semicircle. We'll be in the front of the room. We ask that the teacher stay in the room with us. It's very important for children to see that you support the program. And we ask also that the staff help us with classroom management.

When available, we will have an observer with us as the third member of our team. That person will work with the teacher on any classroom management issues and will participate in some parts of our curriculum.

Teachers are very significant in a child's life. We encourage teachers to make themselves available to children after we are gone, to reinforce the basic concepts in our 2-day presentation. And if a child reports sexual abuse to you, we urge you to believe, thank, and support them for sharing the information. Then you'll need to follow the procedures of the school district to get all of the details and to connect the child with the proper agencies in the system.

We have brought a list of indicators also. These signs, taken by themselves, are not definitive indicators of sexual abuse. However, they do indicate that there might be a problem in some area. There might be problems of family violence or substance abuse. Or the indicators may, in fact, point to child abuse.

We think it's important for people who work with children to be aware of these indicators, and, if you see some signs, pay closer attention. Take the time to ask the child, "Is somebody trying to force or trick you into touch?"

Also, as we said earlier, we give children a card that indicates resources in the community that are available to them. You can remind the child to call any of those numbers or help him or her make the calls.

We also are a resource to you and encourage you to call us if you have a question, or if something comes up and you're not sure what to do next in working with children on these issues. Feel free to call us.

Our presentation is completed. We are open for any questions that you might have about the *Keeping Kids Safe* program, our presentation, your role, or the issue of child sexual abuse.

Reporting Information for Teachers

What Is Reported?

- Physical abuse
- Sexual abuse
- Severe or general neglect
- Willful cruelty toward or unjustifiable punishment of a child
- Cruel and inhuman corporal punishment
- "Unjustifiable" mental suffering
- Any of the above in out-of-home care

Incidents must be reported when they are "observed" OR if there's "reasonable suspicion."

Why Report?

- To protect the child
- To comply with the law
- To get help for the family

Who Reports?

Most professionals who, in the course of their work, come in contact with families and children (medical practitioners, nonmedical practitioners, daycare providers, probation officers, teachers, and social workers) are required to report. Citizens MAY report suspected child abuse if they so choose.

To Whom?

Reports should be made to a "child protective agency," which means police and sheriff's offices, probation offices, or child welfare offices. Check in your county for preferred procedures. Cross-reporting to police occurs in cases of suspected physical and sexual abuse.

When?

A phone report must be made immediately upon suspicion or knowledge. A written report is required within 36 hours. Standardized forms are available from your local reporting agency.

Confidentiality

Confidentiality rules do not apply in child abuse. The confidentiality privilege is superceded by the statutory duty to report.

Liability

You can be held civilly or criminally liable for failing to report suspected child abuse, especially if the child is subsequently hurt.

Immunity

Legally mandated reporters have full immunity. Citizens, when making reports, also have immunity, unless it can be proven that the report was false and the person reporting it knew it was false.

Feedback to Reporter

The child protective agency is required to provide the legally mandated reporter with feedback regarding the investigation and action taken.

Abuse in the Past

The Department of Justice clarifies that reports of abuse must be made at the time the mandated reporter learns of the abuse. There is no statute of limitations in the reporting law; however, most states have differing statutes of limitation regarding prosecution of abuse. If the victim is 18 or over, the child protective authorities will usually refer the case to police for possible assault charges. Criteria for reporting cases involving adults 18 or over include current danger and the presence of other potential victims (such as siblings).

Telling the Client You Are Reporting

You are not legally required to tell the client you are making a report; however, if you foresee a future relationship (as a teacher, therapist, doctor, etc.), it is best to let the client know you are making the referral to child protective services.

Anonymous Reporting

Citizens, if not legally mandated to report, may make anonymous reports. Professionals who are legally mandated to report cannot make anonymous reports.

Parent Meetings

LOGISTICS

The parent meeting should be held approximately 1 week before the children's program is presented. This meeting is usually held at night in order to allow the greatest number of parents to attend. Preparation for the parent meeting includes the following division of responsibilities.

School Administrator's Responsibilities

1. Notify parents of the meeting and encourage them to attend

2. Secure a room for the meeting

3. Provide refreshments, if any

4. Introduce the *Keeping Kids Safe* presenters to parents at the beginning of the meeting

Program Staff's Responsibilities

1. Ask school personnel about the need for translators or other special concerns—if needed, work with the school to get appropriate materials translated

2. Discuss with the principal any concerns about facing parents, such as recent incidents

3. Schedule presenters to conduct the meeting

4. Bring portfolio, handouts, books, and puppets to the meeting

5. Organize the presentation and delineate roles

6. Conduct the meeting

Materials Needed for Parent Meeting

- Handouts (translated where appropriate)
- Permission slips (supplied by school)
- Tapes
- Books

Presentation and Stage Directions

MEETING PREPARATION

1. Place handout materials in an accessible place.

2. Place two chairs in front of the room for presenters.

3. Take posters and touch signs out of the portfolio and place them next to presenters' chairs.

ROOM SETUP

1. Presenters are seated in chairs in front of the room. Project and presenters are introduced by name by the principal (or director, or head teacher).

PARENT PRESENTATION OUTLINE

Introduction

THANK SCHOOL ADMINISTRATOR FOR INTRODUCTION

OVERVIEW OF WHAT WILL BE COVERED

1. Issue of child sexual abuse (statistics and scope of problem)

2. Effects of abuse

3. Why children are vulnerable to abuse

4. Basic *Keeping Kids Safe* concepts

5. Brief overview of the children's program

6. Discussion of resources

7. What parents can do to protect their children from abuse and to reinforce program information

8. Question-and-answer period at end of presentation (questions also will be entertained at any other point during presentation)

Statistics

It is estimated that one in three girls and one in seven boys is sexually abused before the age of 18 (though many experts now think it's closer to one in three girls and one in four boys).

An even more significant statistic is that 75 to 85 percent of the time the person who abuses a child is not a stranger. Rather, it is someone known to the child—someone in the child's support system—such as a family member, friend of the family, neighbor, or babysitter.

Effects on Kids

Sexual abuse can have extremely negative long-term effects on a child.

Children who are sexually abused typically feel guilty. They feel that what happened (the abuse) is their fault, that they caused it, or that they should have stopped it somehow.

Children who have been sexually abused usually feel powerless. Because sexual abuse is primarily an issue of a power imbalance—a bigger, older person taking advantage of a smaller, younger person—children who are being abused often feel that they can do nothing to stop the abuse, that they are helpless.

Children who have been sexually abused are burdened with having to live with a shameful secret. One of the typical features of child sexual abuse is that the child is forced or manipulated into keeping the abuse a secret. This is one of the main clues to the child that something is wrong. The fact that the child is coerced or bribed into secrecy about a touch indicates that the touch is not okay. When the child is touched in an acceptable fashion, there is no pressure to keep the touch a secret. (For example, when a parent tucks a child in at bedtime, there's no instruction to the child to keep the goodnight kiss and hug a secret.)

Victims often feel isolated from their peers. They feel that no one understands. They know that they have had experiences that are different from those of other children.

If the sexual abuse is not treated, the sexually abused child may experience long-term effects. Teenage runaway behavior, teen prostitution, drug and alcohol abuse, depression, and suicide have all been linked to abusive experiences in childhood. The perpetrators of child sexual abuse often have a history of having been sexually abused themselves as children. Furthermore, the ability to trust and to form intimate relationships is often adversely affected in survivors of child sexual abuse. When someone close to a child violates the child's boundaries and trust, it is difficult for the child to trust and become intimate in adult relationships.

Why Children Are Vulnerable

Sexual abuse is fundamentally an issue of power imbalance. We're talking about a bigger person, an older person, taking advantage of a younger, smaller person.

As parents, we know that **we can't possibly supervise children 24 hours a day.** It's just not realistic. We love our kids; we're concerned about them; but we cannot always be there with them to make sure nothing happens. Even when we are there, they can be victimized without our knowledge. So we tend to distance the problem of child sexual abuse. We say that it doesn't happen to our kids; it doesn't happen in neighborhoods like ours; it doesn't happen in schools like ours. We push the problem away because we're not sure just what to do about it. We worry about scaring children or making them uptight about sexuality. So children end up with incomplete information. For example, *we give children a lot of information about strangers.* We tell them, "Don't take candy from strangers," "Don't talk

to strangers," "Don't get in a car with strangers." Kids *should* be informed about possibly dangerous strangers. But strangers are involved in sexual abuse cases less than 25 percent of the time. Thus, *an exclusive focus on "stranger danger" when we talk to children about sexual abuse is unrealistic and inappropriate.*

In addition to telling children about strangers, we give children vague warnings like, "Don't walk through the park," "Don't walk in the dark." This is important. Children must be taught to pay attention to safety conditions. However, we also need to prepare children for the main way in which sexual abuse occurs—someone they know trying to touch them in their private parts. We, as parents, don't teach our children that somebody nice, dressed in an attractive fashion, somebody that they know, could force or trick a child into being touched. Our children are not prepared for and don't know how to prevent sexual abuse as it usually happens.

Basic Keeping Kids Safe Concepts

We view our presentations not as sex education, but, rather, as personal body safety—kind of like traffic safety. When we're training children about crossing the street, we tell them to use the traffic lights and look both ways, not to play in the street. We don't describe to them what they would feel like or look like if they were hit by a truck. Similarly, when we talk about sexual abuse, we talk about it just like any other personal safety issue. That is, we talk to children about uncomfortable situations they might find themselves in. And we brainstorm with them about how they can protect themselves with skills that they already have, like running, yelling, saying no, calling for help, or telling someone they trust.

We teach children about three kinds of touches.

1. The first touch is a **"heart" touch.** That's a touch that *both* people like, that *both* people want.

2. Then there is a **"no" touch.** A "no" touch is a touch that you don't like—a touch that does not feel good to you.

3. Finally there is a **"question mark" touch.** A "question mark" touch is a confusing, mixed-up touch.

We tell children that they have special body rights—that is, they have the right to feel safe, to say "no," and to ask questions if somebody tries to touch them in a way that they don't like.

We tell children that no one has a right to force or trick them into touching private parts of their body or the other person's body.

Highlights of the Keeping Kids Safe *Children's Program*

Children's workshops are held in two sessions, 30 minutes to an hour each, on 2 consecutive days. Presentations are given by a team of two or three trained staff and/or volunteers.

SESSION 1: On the first day, we define sexual abuse and body safety in language the children can understand. For example, the elementary school curriculum defines sexual abuse as "forced or tricked touch to private parts of your body or the other person's body." We identify the private parts of the body. We also identify three special body rights that all children have: the right to be safe, the right to say "no," and the right to ask questions about touches.

Next, we discuss touches that children like ("heart" touches), and dislike ("No" touches), and those touches that are confusing ("?" touches). Presenters do four to six skits designed to illustrate various kinds of touches. With preschool and early elementary school children, colorful, child-sized puppets are used to illustrate and identify touches. Older elementary children identify touches themselves by voting.

In line with our philosophy of never leaving a child in a vulnerable position, each skit identified as showing a "?" or "no" touch is replayed, using children as actors and getting suggestions from the class. In this way, we always model a positive outcome for the children. Skills suggested by the class and presenters are already in a child's repertoire of behavior; they include running away, saying "no" or "stop," and telling someone they trust about the touch (getting help). It is extremely empowering for children to be able to practice prevention skills with their peers in preparation for real-life situations. Since many children blame themselves for the abuse, *we emphasize repeatedly that if a child cannot stop a touch, it is never the child's fault.*

We sing "The Touching Song" with both younger and older children to illustrate the three kinds of touches. We'd like to sing it for you now and do several of our skits to demonstrate our elementary curriculum. We'll start with the Tickle Play and when we're done we'll ask you to vote on what kind of touch it is. Just act like you are members of your children's class. (*Demonstrate the tickle touch. Hold up appropriate touch signs, encouraging parents to vote. Ask what kind of a touch it was. Then ask what a child could do to keep herself safe. Redo skit with positive outcome.*)

Now we're going to show you the Uncle Sam skit. In this skit I'm going to be Uncle Sam. The other presenter will be my niece, Pam, and she's going to be the age of the children in your child's class. We're going to be at a family dinner. Let's see what happens. What kind of touch is this for Pam? (*Demonstrate the Uncle Sam skit. Hold up appropriate touch signs, encouraging parents to vote. Ask what kind of a touch it was. Then ask what Pam could do to keep herself safe. Redo skit with positive outcome. Then sing "The Touching Song.")*

SESSION 2: The concepts presented during Session 1 are reviewed and expanded upon during Session 2. The children are told that sexual abuse can happen anywhere, at any time of the day or night, and to any child, rich or poor, black, brown, or white. We also stress that all kinds of people can sexually abuse children. They may be strangers or people the child knows. In this way, we dispel myths children commonly believe about child sexual abuse.

Next, we introduce the concept of intuition, or funny feelings, the "inner voice" in each of us that warns us something is about to happen. We believe children can employ this internal warning system as another tool to keep themselves safe. Age-appropriate skills are used to show children how they can use their funny feelings. Once again, children replay skits using safety suggestions from presenters and the class.

Now we want to show you a portion of our early elementary curriculum, which teaches the concept of funny feelings to young children. In this skit Yellow Puppet is a little boy who's 6 years old. Purple Puppet is his babysitter, who wants to play a game that gives Johnny a funny feeling. And Safety Friend helps Johnny to identify his funny feelings. (*Demonstrate Funny Feelings skit and redo the skit with positive outcome.*)

Presenters also discuss bribery and give children practice in stranger identification in order to prepare them for possible stranger molestation. Children learn how to do a self-defense yell—a low-pitched, loud yell from deep in the diaphragm that can be used to warn adults that the child needs help or to scare away the potential molester.

Finally, since children are most often molested by someone they know, we include a sequence on incest. Children are shown an initial approach to a daughter by the father, the reaction of an unbelieving mother, and a scene in which the child is believed and gets help. Children are taught new skills to help them deal with the more subtle manipulation by a caretaker or family member. Children are involved, as friends who help the child to tell, in the final skit of this sequence. This allows them to practice newly acquired skills and internalize them for future use.

Private Time

At the end of each session, we offer children a chance to ask us questions and clear up confusion about touches. This portion of the program is called "Private Time" and usually takes place in the 30 minutes immediately following the presentation. We are available to interact with the younger children on a one-to-one basis, reviewing what to do to keep safe and who to tell.

Children who have experienced abuse may approach presenters for help at this time. Children may also go to their parents for help after the presentation. That's why it is important to familiarize yourself with indicators of abuse and available resources. We'll be covering this information in the next portion of our program.

Resources

Before we take questions from the group, we want to briefly review resources that are available to parents. We'll also discuss what parents can do after we have made our classroom presentation to reinforce the information with their own children.

Note to Presenters: *After completion of the description of the children's program, we discuss resources, give out the handouts, and make suggestions about what parents can do after we've made our presentation to the children.*

What Parents Can Do

Parents play a key role in sexual abuse prevention. The main thing parents can do is to keep open lines of communication with their child. Let your child know that he or she can tell you right away if anyone touches his or her private parts.

Some of the possible indicators of sexual abuse include but are not limited to: radical changes in behavior; repeated seductive behavior toward adults; sleep disturbance; child is suddenly more fearful of a person the child formerly liked; excessive sex play; swollen/reddened genitals. These behaviors may signal sexual abuse and, where indicated, the child should be asked matter-of-factly if someone is touching him.

If your child tells you about a sexually abusive touch, give the child your immediate and total support. Let the child know that it is not his or her fault. Tell the child that you believe him or her. We know that children generally don't make up stories about sexual abuse. If you are angry, let the child know that you are angry at the *other person,* not the child.

We are with your children for only a short period of time, so it is very important for you to reinforce the concepts that we have introduced.

Parents can ask their children such questions as:

● Where are your private parts?

● What are the three kinds of touches?

● What kinds of things can people use to bribe kids?

● What can you say, and what can you do, if you get a "no" or "?" touch?

● Who are the different people you can tell?

● What are the two kinds of secrets?

● Is it your fault if a bigger or older person touches you in your private parts?

Reinforce that it is never the child's fault.

Another activity that parents can do with their children is to play "What If?" Ask your child:

● What if the house caught on fire?

● What if I didn't pick you up from school on time?

● What if someone touched you in private parts of your body?

This game allows parents to reinforce general safety concepts and, particularly, to reinforce the message, "come tell me right away if someone touches you in private parts of your body."

Several books have been written about child sexual abuse. They are listed in the *Keeping Kids Safe*: *Family Activity Booklet* (available through PMT Consultants). To help you talk to your child about sexual abuse, we especially recommend the following books:

● *No More Secrets*

● *Come Tell Me Right Away*

● *It's My Body* (for younger children)

Each of these books gives parents ideas about nonthreatening approaches to talking with children about sexual abuse. For a clear explanation of the issue of sexual abuse, we suggest *He Told Me Not to Tell.* A coloring book called *Red Flag Green Flag People* allows parents to work with their child and reinforce concepts about private parts, touches, and safety strategies.

There are several local agencies that provide help for abused children *(provide local resources at this time)*. If you have questions about sexual abuse or other forms of abuse, these are some of the places you can get help in this community.

Our presentation is completed. We are open for any questions that you might have about the *Keeping Kids Safe* program, our presentation, your role, or the issue of child sexual abuse.

Questions Parents Most Frequently Ask

Q. Won't this topic scare young children?

A. No. We've never received a complaint from a parent or teacher after a presentation. As a matter of fact, children are empowered by participating in our program.

Q. Won't this program confuse children about touches? For example, a child won't want her father to kiss her goodnight.

A. Children know the difference between a "heart" touch—such as Daddy kissing them goodnight—and a "question mark" (confusing) or "no" touch. One way a child can tell is that when Daddy kisses her goodnight he does not tell her to keep the kiss a secret.

Q. What kind of people do this?

A. Offenders, as we've said before, come from all racial, class, and ethnic groups. There are different theories as to why a person becomes an offender. We know that most offenders were themselves abused physically and/or sexually as children and that 95 percent of abusers are men.

Q. What if a child says someone is touching her?

A. Believe the child. Thank the child for telling you. Tell the child that you will do everything you can to get the abuse to stop. Then follow the local procedure for getting the details and making the report, if this is indicated.

Q. What should I say to my child?

A. You should tell your child that he has the right to decide about touches, especially to private parts of his body, and that no one has the right to force or trick him into touching. Also, you should reinforce his or her right to say "no." The main thing to tell your child is that, if someone tries to or actually does touch him in private parts of his body, the child should tell you right away.

Q. Is this happening more now than before?

A. Sexual abuse of children has been going on for centuries. We don't know if it's happening more now than before. What we do know is that people (especially adult survivors of incest) have been talking more openly about it in the past few years and that media attention has focused on it. So we are definitely hearing more about it.

Q. Wouldn't it do more damage to report abuse and risk breaking up a family?

A. No. The most important thing is to stop the abuse and protect the child. The question of whether or not the family stays together would be decided by the criminal justice system, the family itself, and professionals working with the offender and family to implement a treatment plan.

Q. Children have active imaginations—couldn't they falsely accuse someone if they were angry at that person?

A. Ninety-nine percent of the time children don't lie about sexual abuse. Children don't know what will happen once they report sexual abuse; the outcome is very unpredictable. So, there is no immediate advantage in inventing an accusation. Further, the child doesn't know in advance who will be removed from the situation, or whether other adults will believe her. This is not the type of problem that offers a child hope for a positive reward, or even positive attention from adults.

Q. How can you tell if a child is being abused?

A. You can't always tell by looking whether a child is being abused. There are, however, some indicators that reflect something is wrong (see pages 22–24). The "something wrong" might be sexual abuse. It is important for adults to consider sexual abuse as one of the potential sources of trouble for children.

Criteria for Success

- Decide what success means for your program.

- Decide what success will be for children, parents, teachers, the community, and the school system.

- Know that in each area success will be different, come in different ways, and be accepted differently.

- Think about different ways success can be defined, reported, shared, and documented.

SIGNS OF SUCCESS WITH CHILDREN

- When they know the song at the end of 2 days

- When they're smiling and singing out loud

- When they come up after a class and hug you and say, "That's a 'heart' touch"

- When you have to say "Hi!" a hundred times on your way into a school

- When they see you on the street and say, "It's the touching lady" or "It's the safety people"

- When they hang on the fence as you're leaving

- When they expand on your information and ask you more questions

- When you see them practicing keeping an arm's distance away or the self-defense yell

- When they come to Private Time and share anything! (Each child's problems are big problems to him or her.)

- When children disclose: when they learn they can say "no," that no one has the right to touch them, and that there is someone they can trust and tell

- And, of course, you will develop your own criteria for success as you become more experienced with presenting the program.

SIGNS OF SUCCESS WITH PARENTS

- When they share their own experiences of sexual abuse during a parent meeting

- When they give positive testimonials at a parent meeting about their children—or friends' children, attending other schools—who have been through the program

- When they smile and nod their heads during a parent meeting

- When they are upset because a meeting is over

- When they have a hundred more questions to ask and it's 10:00 P.M.

- When they're upset because you can't go to their child's class or school

- When they want to volunteer with your program

- When they give you a donation at the end of the meeting

- When they call you or speak to you about a report

- When they ask for a referral

- When they go to the principal and demand that your program be allowed to happen

SIGNS OF SUCCESS WITH TEACHERS

- When a teacher asks you to come to his or her school

- When a teacher takes information to the principal and "pleads your case"

- When most teachers are smiling at the end of a staff meeting

- When they have sincere questions at the end of a staff meeting

- When they sit attentively through your program

- When they have the room set up for you when you arrive

- When they offer you coffee in the morning

- When they help you with the preparations for your presentation and Private Time

- When you get letters from a class after you've been to a school

- When missing recess or being a little late to lunch is not so important

- When they make a place for you to do Private Time

- When they share their concerns about children with you tactfully

- When they tell other teachers about how wonderful your program is

- When they ask for resources and follow-up curriculum materials

SIGNS OF SUCCESS WITH THE COMMUNITY

- When you have more requests for presentations than you can handle

- When you have more requests for community education than you can handle

- When the media can't get enough of your program

- When it feels like you're on someone's list of who to call about anything having to do with sexual abuse

SIGNS OF SUCCESS WITH THE SYSTEM

- When they think it's your program's fault they're getting so many reports

- When they call you by your first name

- When they thank you for a report

- When they call you for more information about a report

- When they give you follow-up information

- When they acknowledge your presence in public

- When they acknowledge your professional ability

- When they invite you to sit in on an interview with them

- When you finally learn who's doing what and who's who

- When you finally learn who should be doing what

- When people stop asking you what you're doing there and start expecting that you'll be there

- In this area success is going to be very different for each system, and so each program's success depends on many things:

  - What role your program takes in the system

  - To what extent your program is a child advocacy program

  - How closely related to the existing system your program is

  - How well you know and are known by the system

  - How well the system has been able to do their job in the past

  - How much the system was involved in the development of your program

  - How much your program has to relate to the system

  - How many people and which ones in the system are supportive of your program

Part 2 — Curricula

Introduction

The curricula are divided into two sections. Chapter 5 contains the Early Childhood Curriculum for children ages 3 to 7 in preschool through second grade. Chapter 6 is comprised of the Elementary Curriculum for children ages 8 to 11 in third through fifth grade. Within these two chapters, the curricula are further subdivided into lessons that include objectives, activities, and facilitators' notes. These lessons can be used as a whole or as separate modules to allow greater flexibility in scheduling the program, depending on time constraints. If the presenters have limited time, they may choose to do one or two activities from a session on one day and subsequent activities at another time. Each activity generally takes 10 to 20 minutes to present.

When used as a whole, the Early Childhood Curriculum is intended to be delivered in two 30- to 45-minute sessions over a 2-day period. The Elementary Curriculum is presented in two 45-minute to an hour segments on 2 separate days. For ease in role-playing and use of the puppets, two prevention educators are needed to present the material to the children. However, when budgeting allows, it is helpful to have an observer also. (Refer to "Role of the Observer" in the chapter on Classroom Management.)

5

Early Childhood Curriculum

Session 1

. . . .

ACTIVITY 1

Purpose: Introductions and special rules

Note: Presenters sit on chairs in front of the children with three chairs of puppets behind them. Observer sits at the end of the semicircle closest to Presenter 2.

OBJECTIVES: By the end of Activity 1, the children will have learned ground rules and definitions of personal safety and the private parts of the body.

Introduction

[*Presenter 1: Have the children sit on chairs in a semicircle.*]

[*Put on the children's name tags. All adults in the room also get name tags.*]

PRESENTER 1: [*Introduces Self, Co-Presenter, Observer, and Visitors.*] We're from the *Keeping Kids Safe* program. We're going to be talking to you about some very important things today, but first I want to tell you about our ground rules, so that everyone can hear.

1. The first rule is: **one person talks at a time.** When we are talking, you are listening. And when you talk, we will listen to you. It's very important to listen.

2. **If you have something to say, raise your hand.** Can everyone raise their hands now to show you know what that means? That's right. You can put your hands down now. We call on quiet hands.

3. When we're finished today, we'll be around for a while longer. If you have something you'd like to ask us or tell us, you can do that by yourself then. We call this Private Time.

Definition

PRESENTER 1: We're here to talk about how to keep yourself safe when someone touches you in private parts of your body and it makes you feel funny or you don't like it. We're also going to talk about when someone wants you to touch them in their private parts and you don't want to.

Definition—Private Parts

PRESENTER 1: Your private parts are here, here, here, and here: [*Point to lips, chest, crotch, and rear*] the mouth, the chest, between the legs, and the bottom. Let's all stand up now and point to our private parts. You can sit down now.

ACTIVITY 2

OBJECTIVES: By the end of Activity 2, the children will have learned about body ownership, and the concept of private body parts will be reinforced.

PRESENTER 1: This is **Safety Friend,** who wants to tell you something very important. Can you say hello to Safety Friend? [*Puppet says hello and waves.*]

Intro: *Safety Friend*

Your Body Is Your Own

SAFETY FRIEND (PRESENTER 2): Every kid is different and special. One thing that makes us special is that **we all own our own bodies.** Your body is your own special property. We think that no one should touch you in private parts of your body or ask you to touch them in their private parts, if it makes you feel funny, or you don't like it.

Here's a picture of me. **Let's find the private parts on Safety Friend's picture.** [*Show Poster: "Safety Friend"*]

Concept: *My body belongs to me*

Show Poster: *"Safety Friend"*

"SAFETY FRIEND" POSTER — FRONT

"SAFETY FRIEND" POSTER — BACK

Show Poster: "Safe Scenes"
Point to children feeling safe.

"SAFE SCENES" POSTER

PRESENTER 1: Is the hair a private part? No!

[*Safety Friend shakes head and says "No!" Presenter 1 points to private parts and nonprivate parts on Safety Friend's picture. Safety Friend puppet gestures and says "yes" or "no" for each body part.*]

PRESENTER 1: Is the mouth a private part? Yes! That's a private part on everyone's body.

[*Safety Friend nods head and says, "Yes!"*]

PRESENTER 1: Is the hand a private part? No! Is the chest a private part? Yes! That's a private part on everyone's body. Is the knee a private part? No! Is the toe a private part? No! Is between the legs a private part? Yes! That's a private part on everyone's body. Here's the back of Safety Friend. Is the back of the head a private part? No! Is the heel a private part? No! Is the bottom a private part? Yes! That's a private part on everyone's body. **Remember, no one should touch you in private parts of your body if it feels funny or you don't like it.**

ACTIVITY 3

OBJECTIVES: By the end of Activity 3, the children will have learned the concept of body safety.

Personal Body Safety

PRESENTER 1: Every child should feel safe. Feeling safe feels warm inside and out. **Feeling safe feels like no one can hurt you.**

All of these children feel safe. This child feels safe when he's with his parents. This child feels safe with her whole family. This child feels safe when she's by herself. We're going to tell you how you can feel safe, even when you're all by yourself. You don't have to be Wonder Woman or Superman to feel safe when you're by yourself. How can you tell these children feel safe? They're all smiling and looking happy.

ACTIVITY 4

OBJECTIVES: By the end of Activity 4, children will have learned to identify "heart," "question mark," and "no" touches, and will have learned at least three safe-keeping strategies for when they're confronted with a "?" or a "no" touch.

Talking about Touching

PRESENTER 2: Now we want you to meet three more friends of ours. This is Yellow Puppet. Say hello to Yellow Puppet! [*Yellow Puppet greets children.*]

PRESENTER 1: This is Green Puppet. Say hello to Green Puppet! [*Green Puppet greets children.*] This is Purple Puppet. Say hello to Purple Puppet! [*Purple Puppet greets children.*]

PRESENTER 2: Now Yellow Puppet wants to tell you about the three kinds of touches.

YELLOW PUPPET (PRESENTER 2): We think there are three kinds of touches. The first kind of touch is a **"heart" touch.** That's a touch that feels good and safe. It's a touch that **both people like and both people want.** [*Puppet holds up "heart" touch sign while speaking.*] The next kind of touch is a **"no" touch**. You do not like this kind of touch. You want a "no" touch to stop. [*Puppet holds up "no" touch sign.*] Then there's a **"question mark" or "I don't know" touch.** A "?" touch is a mixed-up touch. It's kind of confusing. You may want it at first, but then change your mind. Or you may like the person who's doing the touching, but you may not like how the touch feels.

PRESENTER 1: Now we're going to sing a song about the three kinds of touches. And when you learn the song, you can sing it with us.

Tickle Play

All three puppets sing chorus and first verse of "The Touching Song"

Chorus
There are three kinds of touches, this we know—
A "heart," a "question mark," and "no."
"No" means "stop,"

Presenter 2 = Yellow Puppet (child)

Presenter 1 = Purple and Green Puppets

Concept: "Heart," "no," and "?" touches

"THE TOUCHING SONG"

"Heart" means "go,"
"Question mark" means "I don't know."

First verse
Now if I tickle you and you say "no"
And I don't stop, where should you go?
You could go and tell somebody you know
And keep very safe from the tickle-o.

Note: *Make Yellow Puppet's age the same as the kids' age*

YELLOW PUPPET [*Introduces Tickle Play*]: Now we're going to do a play for you. I'm going to be a girl named Sherry; I am _____ years old. Purple Puppet is my big sister Mary; she's 8 years old. Watch and see what happens.

PURPLE: Hi, Sherry!

YELLOW: Hi, Mary!

PURPLE: Want to play a game with me?

YELLOW: What kind of game?

PURPLE: It's the tickle game. Ready?

YELLOW: Okay!

PURPLE: Tickle, tickle, tickle!

[*Purple Puppet tickles Yellow Puppet under her arms. Yellow puppet doesn't like it and tries to move away.*]

Presenters: *Remember to slow down the action. Show emotion on your faces.*

GREEN PUPPET (PRESENTER 1): What kind of touch was that for Yellow Puppet? Let's ask and find out. Yellow Puppet, did you like that touch? [*Green holds up each touch sign in order ("heart," "no," "?")*]

YELLOW PUPPET (PRESENTER 2): No, I did not like that touch.

GREEN: Then that was not a "heart" touch. Was that a "no" touch, Yellow Puppet?

YELLOW: That was a "no" touch. I wanted that touch to stop. I did not like that touch.

GREEN: Could that have been a "?" touch, too?

YELLOW: Yes, it was. At first I wanted to play the tickle game, but then I didn't like it when my sister would not stop tickling me. I changed my mind!

GREEN: You can change your mind about a touch! And not everyone likes to be tickled. If you don't like a touch or it feels funny, you can do something to keep safe.

PRESENTER 1: Now let's see what Yellow Puppet does to keep safe when she gets a "no" or "?" touch. Let's listen to the song again and find out.

ALL THREE PUPPETS sing the tickle verse only.

[**Redo skit** with "keep safe" positive outcome (say "no" and tell).]

YELLOW PUPPET (PRESENTER 2): This time I'm going to be ___ years old again. I'm Sherry and that's my big sister Mary. [*Points to Purple Puppet.*]

PURPLE: Hi! Want to play a game with me, Sherry?

YELLOW: Okay, what kind of game is it?

PURPLE: It's called the tickle game. Ready? Tickle, tickle, tickle.

[*Purple tickles Yellow. Yellow puts hand out and moves away.*]

YELLOW: Stop it! I do not like that. [*Goes to Observer and says*] Mommy, Mary's tickling me and she won't stop.

OBSERVER: I'm glad you told me, Sherry. We are going to get that touch to stop.

PRESENTER 1: What did Yellow Puppet do to keep safe? Yes, she said, "Stop it!" and she told her Mommy. That's what you can do, too. Is there anyone who would like to come up with the puppets and practice keeping safe from the tickle touch?

Note: The Observer sits at the end of the semicircle and models a supportive adult in re-dos with puppets and kids.

TICKLE TOUCH PLAY

Remember: *When choosing children to act in the skits, alternate between boys and girls and pick children of different races. Pick two helpers per skit with older kids; one per skit with younger kids.*

Note: *4- to 5-year-olds can be asked what the child or puppet did to keep safe.*

Presenter 1 = Purple and Green
Presenter 2 = Yellow

Presenters: *Show emotions on your faces*

[Yellow Puppet helps child decide what he or she will do to keep safe as the group watches.]

YELLOW: Can you say "no" or "stop" and tell _____ (teacher, observer, aide)? Okay, let's watch what _____ does to keep safe.

[Purple Puppet tickles child. Yellow Puppet prompts child to say "no" and tell.]

[Observer leads applause when the child finishes.]

[Yellow Puppet states or asks what the child did to keep safe.]

PRESENTER 1: Now we're going to sing about another kind of touch. You can sing with us if you like.

*[**All three puppets** sing chorus and second (Bully) verse.]*

> ### Chorus
> There are three kinds of touches, this we know—
> A "heart," a "question mark," and "no."
> "No" means "stop,"
> "Heart" means "go,"
> "Question mark" means "I don't know."
>
> ### Bully verse
> **What if a bully pushes you down**
> **And there's nobody else around?**
> **You can run for help because, you see,**
> **That's a "no" touch, we all agree.**

YELLOW PUPPET: *[Introduces Bully Play]* This time I'm going to be a boy named Peter and I'm ___ years old. I am waiting for my daddy to pick me up from school. Purple Puppet is a big kid that I don't know. Watch and see what happens.

PURPLE: Hey kid! Move! Get lost! Beat it! This is my spot!

[Yellow stands in front of children. Purple pushes Yellow away and stands in Yellow's place. Yellow moves away, with head down, looking sad.]

GREEN: What kind of touch was that for Yellow Puppet? Let's ask him and find out. Yellow Puppet, did you like that touch?

YELLOW: No, I did not like that touch at all! I wanted that bully to quit pushing me!

GREEN: So that was a "no" touch, huh? [*Holds up "no" touch sign.*]

YELLOW: Uh huh! It sure was!

GREEN: That's what we call a "no" touch. That's a touch you don't like and want to stop.

PRESENTER 1: Now let's see what Yellow Puppet does to keep safe when he gets a "no" touch. Listen and find out.

[***All three puppets*** *sing the Bully verse.*]

> **What if a bully pushes you down**
> **And there's nobody else around?**
> **You can run for help because, you see,**
> **That's a "no" touch, we all agree.**

Redo skit with "keep safe" positive outcome (say "no," tell someone, and keep an arm's distance).

YELLOW: I'm the boy who's waiting for my dad to pick me up at school again. Watch what I do this time.

PURPLE: Hey kid! Move . . . [*tries to push Yellow*].

YELLOW: Stop! Don't push me! I was standing here first. [*Moves away, keeping an arm's distance. Stands in front of observer.*] Teacher, that bully was pushing me!

OBSERVER: I'm glad you told me. We will get that touch to stop.

Observer: *Models supportive adult*

PRESENTER 1: What did Yellow Puppet do to keep safe this time? Raise your hand if you know. Yes, he told that bully to stop and he told his teacher. Yellow Puppet did something else to keep safe. He kept an arm's distance. Watch again.

[*Purple tries to push Yellow, but Yellow moves away.*]

PRESENTER 1: What's Yellow Puppet doing? He's moving away from a touch that doesn't feel safe. That's something you can do too. It's called "keeping an arm's distance." Would someone like to come up and practice keeping safe from a bully touch?

[*Yellow Puppet helps child decide what he or she will do to keep safe.*]

YELLOW PUPPET: Can you say "no" or "stop" and tell a teacher? Can you keep an arm's distance, too? I'll help you! Okay, let's watch what _____ does to keep safe.

[*Purple Puppet tries to push child. Yellow Puppet helps child say "no," tell the observer, and keep an arm's distance.*]

[*Observer leads applause when the child finishes.*]

[*Yellow Puppet states what the child did to keep safe.*]

Aunt Janie Touch

[**All three puppets** *sing chorus and third (Aunt Janie) verse.*]

> **Chorus**
> There are three kinds of touches, this we know—
> A "heart," a "question mark," and "No."
> "No" means "stop,"
> "Heart" means "go,"
> "Question mark" means "I don't know."
>
> **Aunt Janie verse**
> **You see Aunt Janie only once a year**
> **And when she finally does appear,**
> **She gives you a "heart" touch, that's very clear.**
> **We can see you grin from ear to ear!**

[*Yellow Puppet introduces play.*]

YELLOW PUPPET: This time I'm a(n) _____-year-old boy named Tommy. Green Puppet will be my Aunt Janie. She is going to come visit me. Watch and see what happens.

GREEN: La-la-la; La-la-la! [*Knock, knock, knock!*]

Presenter 1 = *Purple and Green*
Presenter 2 = *Yellow*

**AUNT JANIE PLAY—
HEART TOUCH**

YELLOW: [*Sitting on floor, playing with toys*] Who is it?

GREEN: It's your Aunt Janie!

YELLOW: [*Calls out*] Mom, it's Aunt Janie! [*Opens door*] Hi! How are you?

GREEN: Hi! Good to see you, Tommy!

[*Yellow sits on floor with toys in front of the children. When Green knocks, Yellow opens door and gets and gives a big hug from Green. Both look happy.*]

GREEN PUPPET: What kind of touch was that for Yellow Puppet? Yellow Puppet, did you like that touch?

YELLOW: Yes, I liked it and I wanted my Aunt Janie to hug me. It was a "heart" touch for me. I liked it and wanted it too.

GREEN: A "heart" touch is a touch that both people like. It's a safe touch.

[*Green Puppet holds up appropriate touch sign "Heart."*]

PRESENTER 1: Who would like to come up and get a "heart" touch from Aunt Janie? Who hasn't had a turn?

[*Yellow Puppet coaches the child.*]

YELLOW: Okay, you'll be sitting here playing with your toys and Aunt Janie is going to knock on the door. Can you say, "Who is it?" and then open the door and get a "heart" touch from Aunt Janie? Okay!

GREEN: [*Hums ("la-la-la"), knocks on door, and, when child asks who it is and opens door, gives child a hug. Holds up "heart" touch sign.*]

[*Observer leads applause when the child finishes.*]

Uncle Sam Touch

PRESENTER 1: Now we're going to sing about one more touch. Sing with us!

Concept: *Modeling safety skill of finding out who's knocking and getting parent's permission before opening the door*

Presenters: *Show happiness on your faces*

Note: *No re-do with puppets in this skit*

Remember: *Some children may be shy. Never force a hug.*

UNCLE SAM TOUCH SKIT

Presenter 1 = *Purple and Green*

Presenter 2 = *Yellow*

Presenters: *Show emotions on your faces*

[**All three puppets** *sing chorus and fourth (Uncle Sam) verse.*]

> ***Chorus***
> There are three kinds of touches, this we know—
> A "heart," a "question mark," and "no."
> "No" means "stop,"
> "Heart" means "go,"
> "Question mark" means "I don't know."
>
> ***Uncle Sam verse***
> **When you sit on his lap**
> **Your Uncle Sam**
> **Is sweet and tender as a lamb.**
> **But if "lamb-Sam" touches you where you don't like,**
> **You can tell him to "go take a hike!"**

[*Yellow Puppet introduces play.*]

YELLOW: I'm going to be a girl named Pam and I am ___ years old. Purple Puppet is my Uncle Sam. We're at a family dinner. Watch and see what happens.

PURPLE: Hi, Pam!

YELLOW: Hi, Uncle Sam!

PURPLE: Come sit on your Uncle Sam's lap.

YELLOW: Okay! [*Happy and smiling*]

PURPLE: What a pretty girl you are getting to be. Oh, I love to hold you on my lap and squeeze you real tight! It's so great to see you! [*Rubs her all over.*]

[*Yellow squirms and looks unhappy. Position Purple on Presenter 1's leg. Purple pats Presenter's leg when asking Yellow to sit on his lap. Yellow willingly sits on Uncle Sam's lap (on Presenter 1's leg in front of Purple). Purple squeezes Yellow and touches her all over her body. Yellow looks uncomfortable, squirms, and leans away.*]

GREEN: What kind of touch was that for Yellow Puppet? Was it a "heart" touch for you, Pam?

YELLOW: No, it was not a "heart" touch. I did not like that touch.

GREEN: Was it a "no" touch?

YELLOW: Yes, it was a "no" touch. I did not like it when my uncle was squeezing me too tight and touching me all over. I wanted that touch to stop!

GREEN: Could that have been a "?" touch too?

YELLOW: Yes. At first I wanted to sit on my Uncle Sam's lap. I really like my uncle, but I didn't like the way he was touching me.

GREEN: You can like the person, but you may not always like the touch.

PRESENTER 1: What can Yellow Puppet do to keep safe when she gets a "no" or "?" touch? Let's listen and find out.

[**All three puppets** slowly sing Uncle Sam verse only.]

[Redo skit with "keep safe" positive outcome (say "no," get off lap, and tell).]

YELLOW: I'm at a family dinner with my Uncle Sam again. Watch what I do this time.

PURPLE: Hi, Pam!

YELLOW: Hi, Uncle Sam!

PURPLE: Come sit on your Uncle Sam's lap. [Pats leg.]

YELLOW: Okay! [Sits on lap, looks happy.]

PURPLE: What a pretty girl you are getting to be. I just love to hold you on my lap and squeeze you real tight! It's so great to see you. [Squeezes and rubs her all over.]

YELLOW: Stop it! No! I like you, but I do not like it when you touch me like that. [Gets off Uncle Sam's lap and speaks to audience.] I'm going to tell my mom and dad what just happened.

Note: Omit singing the verse if the children are restless. Instead, state what the child can do to keep safe and then demonstrate.

Concept: It's never the child's fault.

Emphasize: If a child can't stop a touch, it's never the child's fault. It's always the fault of the person who's doing the touching.

Concept: Three kinds of touches

PRESENTER 1: What did Pam do this time to keep herself safe? Raise your hand if you know. Yes, she said, "Stop it! No!" and got off her uncle's lap. And who was she going to tell? Yes, Daddy and Mommy. Would someone who hasn't had a turn like to come up and practice keeping safe?

[*Yellow Puppet helps child decide what he or she will do to keep safe.*]

YELLOW: Can you say "no" or "stop" to Uncle Sam? Can you get off his lap? And who can you tell? Okay. Let's watch what _____ does to keep safe.

[*Have child sit on Presenter 1's lap in front of Purple puppet. Yellow puppet stands close by and helps child say "no," get off lap, and tell someone about the touch.*]

[*Observer leads applause when the child finishes.*]

[*Yellow Puppet states what the child did to keep safe.*]

ACTIVITY 5

OBJECTIVES: By the end of Activity 5, the children will have reviewed the concepts learned in Activities 1 through 4.

Review

PRESENTER 1: Let's remember what we talked about today.

[*Presenter 1 reviews private parts: have children come up and point to private parts on Safety's picture or have children stand up and point to their private parts. Review definition of sexual abuse.*]

PRESENTER 2: We think if a child gets a "no" or "?" touch and can't stop it, it's never the child's fault. Whose fault is it? It's always the fault of the older or bigger person touching you.

PRESENTER 1: If you get a "no" or "?" touch, we think it's important to tell somebody, so that they can help you keep safe. You can tell your mommy or daddy. Who else can you tell? Here's what Yellow Puppet and you can do to keep safe if you get a "no" or "?" touch. [*Presenter 2 uses Yellow Puppet to act* out each skill, relating back to the skits, when Presenter 1 states them.] **Tell somebody you trust** [*Yellow Puppet tells Mom about the tickle touch.*] **Say "no" or "stop!"** [*Yellow Puppet says "no" to Uncle Sam.*] **Call for help** [*Yellow Puppet calls for teacher's help with the bully.*] **Keep an arm's distance** [*Yellow Puppet demonstrates.*] **Run away or walk away** [*Yellow Puppet runs away.*]

PRESENTER 2: Let's all sing the first part of "The Touching Song" (chorus only).

ACTIVITY 6

OBJECTIVES: To give children the opportunity for a one-on-one session to review concepts, to talk about uncomfortable touches, and to get help in getting touches to stop.

Private Time

PRESENTER 1: After we've finished, if you want to talk with us about the plays, songs, or different kinds of touches, we'll be here for a little longer. You can talk to us privately by yourself if you want to. And we'll be back again tomorrow to tell you some more things you can do to keep yourself safe.

Notes: *Sections 1 through 4 of the Review can be abbreviated with younger children whose attention span is limited. Remember in an abbreviated version to stress saying "no," telling someone, and that it's never the child's fault. Also, have children stand up together and point to their private parts.*

Purpose: *Introduction and special rules*

Note: *Presenters sit on two chairs in front, with three chairs behind them for puppets*

Presenter 1 = Purple and Green Puppets

Presenter 2 = Yellow and Safety Puppets

Session 2

[Observer sits at end of semicircle closest to Presenter 2.]

Introduction

[Have the children sit on chairs in a semicircle.]

[Put on children's name tags. All adults in room also get name tags.]

PRESENTER 1: *[Introduces Self, Co-Presenter, Observer, and Visitors.]* We're from the *Keeping Kids Safe* program. We're back again today to tell you some more ways you can keep yourself safe, but first let's remember our ground rules, so that everyone can hear.

1. Remember that **one person talks at a time.** When we are talking, you are listening. And when you talk we will listen to you. It's very important to listen.

2. If you have something to say or tell us, **raise your hand** just like you did yesterday. We call on quiet hands.

3. We'll be here again, when we're finished, for Private Time. If you have a question you'd like to ask us, or if you'd like to talk to us by yourself, you can do that then.

<u>ACTIVITY 1</u>

OBJECTIVES: By the end of Activity 1, children will have reviewed the concepts learned in Activities 2 through 5 in Session 1.

Review

PRESENTER 2: *[Reintroduces the puppets.]* Remember our puppets? Here's Yellow Puppet. Can you say hello? *[Puppet says hello.]*

PRESENTER 1: Here's Green Puppet.

GREEN PUPPET: Hi everybody!

PRESENTER 2: And here's Purple Puppet who'd like to say hello, hello, hello!

YELLOW PUPPET (PRESENTER 2): Let's sing our touching song together. [*Sing "The Touching Song."*]

SAFETY FRIEND (PRESENTER 2): Remember Safety Friend? Safety says, "Hi girls and boys!" Let's find the private parts on Safety Friend's picture. [*Presenter 1 holds up "Safety Friend" poster and four children come up, one at a time, to point to a private part on the poster.*]

PRESENTER 1: Now let's all stand up and point to our private parts. Remember that **no one should touch a child on their private parts** if it feels funny or the child doesn't like it.

PRESENTER 1: Remember the "heart" touch, the "no" touch, and the "?" touch? Remember, a **"heart" touch is a touch that both people like** and want. A "no" touch is a touch that you don't like and that you'd like to stop. **And a "?" touch is a confusing, mixed-up touch.** You may like it at first, but then you may change your mind, or you may like the person but not the touch. What can you do to keep safe if you get a "no" or a "?" touch? [*To prompt kids, mention a skill, like: you could call for help*.] **And what can you say to get a touch to stop? ("no," "stop")**

PRESENTER 2: Who can you tell? [*Mom, Dad, uncle, grandparents, teacher, etc.*]

PRESENTER 2: And if a child can't stop a touch, **it's never the child's fault.** It's always the fault of the bigger or older person who's doing the touching.

ACTIVITY 2

OBJECTIVES: By the end of Activity 2 children will have learned that children can be touched in their private parts anywhere, any time of the day or night; that anyone can touch them; and that it can happen to any child. Private parts touching is never the child's fault.

Show Poster: "Safety Friend"

"SAFETY FRIEND" POSTER — FRONT

"SAFETY FRIEND" POSTER — BACK

Observer: *Leads applause after each child comes up and after the group points to their private parts*

Note: *Show touch signs in order*

"THE TOUCHING SONG" WITH SIGNS

Show Poster: *"Any Kind of Child." Point to different kids.*

"ANY KIND OF CHILD" POSTER

Show Poster: *"Where It Can Happen." Point to different places.*

"WHERE IT CAN HAPPEN" POSTER

Show Poster: *"When It Can Happen." Point to different activities around the clock.*

"WHEN IT CAN HAPPEN" POSTER

Concept: *Never the child's fault.*

Myths and Facts

PRESENTER 2: All kinds of kids might be touched in private parts of their bodies in a way they don't like or that makes them feel funny. It can be a girl who looks like this, a boy who looks like that, a baby, a big kid, or a little kid.

Children can get touched in their private parts when they don't like it in **many different places.** Let's find all the different places children can be when they get touched. Children might be touched when they are at home. Where else? Who can raise their hand and tell me another place where children might be touched in private parts of their bodies? Yes, children might be touched at school, in a park, at a store, in a car, on a bus, or in the street. It can happen anywhere.

PRESENTER 1: Children can be touched in their private parts in a way that makes them feel funny **at any time of the day or night.** Or they might be asked to touch someone else in their private parts at any time. It could happen while a child is sleeping. When else? Could it happen when a child is getting ready to go out? Yes. How about when a child's at school in the morning? Yes. How about when a child's walking to or from school in the middle of the day? Yes. Children can be touched in their private parts in the middle of the day. How about in the afternoon when a child's at the playground? Yes. It could even happen in the evening, before or after dinner. Or when a child's taking a bath and getting ready for bed at night, the child might be touched in private parts of the body in a way that feels funny. It can happen any time of the day or night.

All kinds of people might touch kids in their private parts in a way that the child doesn't like. Or they might ask a child to touch them in their private parts in a way that feels funny. It can be a woman, a man, older people, younger people, people who wear uniforms, people who wear suits, strangers, or people you know. We know there are **two kinds of people** who touch children in private parts of their bodies when they don't like it or it feels funny: **strangers** (people you don't know) and **people you know.**

And if a child is touched in private parts and doesn't want to be, **it's never the child's fault.** It's always the fault of the older or bigger person who's touching the child or asking the child to touch him or her.

ACTIVITY 3

OBJECTIVES: By the end of Activity 3, the children will have learned to identify their funny feelings, and to use these funny feelings in keeping themselves safe.

Funny Feelings

SAFETY FRIEND (PRESENTER 1): Yesterday we talked about how you can keep yourself safe when you get a "no" or "?" touch. Today we're going to talk about other things you can do to keep safe when someone wants to touch you in private parts of your body or wants you to touch them in their private parts, and you don't like it or it make you feel funny. Now we want to tell you about something else you can use to keep yourself safe, something called a "funny feeling." A funny feeling is a little voice inside of you that tells you that something is about to happen . . . that maybe something's not okay. It's like the little voice is saying, **"Uh-oh! Uh-oh!"** [*jumping up and down*] **"Better say no!"** We think it's important to listen to your funny feelings. Listening to the little "uh-oh" voice inside of you can help you keep safe.

SAFETY (PRESENTER 1): [*Jumping up and down*] Here's a song about funny feelings.

YELLOW (PRESENTER 2): [*To Safety Friend*] What's a funny feeling?

SAFETY: Well, I'll tell you.

"The Funny Feelings Song"

Verse
A funny feeling's a voice inside you,
It's there to help you,
It's there to guide you,
And if you listen, the voice will go:
Uh-oh! Better say no!
Uh-oh! Better say no!

Chorus
Better say no! Better say no!
And if you listen, the voice will go:
Uh-oh! Better say no!
[*Slower.*] **Uh-oh! Better say no!**

Show Poster: "Potential Offenders." Point to different adults.

"POTENTIAL OFFENDERS" POSTER

Presenter 1 = Safety
Presenter 2 = Yellow

Note: *Both Presenters sing; the puppets hold hands and sway back and forth. Safety jumps up and down when saying "uh-oh!"*

"THE FUNNY FEELINGS SONG"

Note: *Yellow Puppet sets up the play and assigns roles. The age of the child will vary depending on the age of the group.*

Concept: *Bribe*

Concept: *Trust your feelings.*

Note: *Presenter 2 uses both Safety and Yellow puppets at the same time in re-do (one on each hand). Safety is held at Yellow's shoulder like a conscience figure.*

Note: *Each time Yellow hears the "uh-oh!" voice, he moves to the front and speaks directly to the children.*

YELLOW PUPPET (PRESENTER 2): Now we are going to do a play about a little boy who gets a funny feeling about something his babysitter asks him to do. I'm going to be the little boy named Johnny. I'm ___ years old. Purple Puppet is my babysitter. Let's see what happens.

PURPLE PUPPET (PRESENTER 1): It's story time Johnny! Go pick out your favorite story.

YELLOW: Okay! [*Starts to leave*]

PURPLE: But wait a minute Johnny. Come back! Today we're going to do something different. This time I want you to take off all your clothes, and I'll take off all my clothes, and we can touch each other while we read the story. Doesn't that sound like fun?

PURPLE: It'll be okay Johnny. I'll tell you what: if you take off your clothes and let me touch you, I'll give you all the cookies you can eat. [*Rubs tummy*]

YELLOW: [*Reluctantly*] Cookies? Well, okay.

SAFETY FRIEND (PRESENTER 2): Johnny had a lot of funny feelings about what his babysitter asked him to do. Watch me this time to see when Johnny gets a funny feeling. Listen for the "Uh-oh" voice, and watch what Johnny does to keep safe.

Redo Play

PURPLE: It's story time Johnny! Go pick out your favorite story.

YELLOW: Okay! [*Starts to leave*]

PURPLE: But wait a minute, Johnny. Come back! Today we're going to do something different. This time I want you to take off all your clothes, and I'll take off all my clothes, and we can touch each other while we read the story. Doesn't that sound like fun?

SAFETY FRIEND: Uh-oh! Uh-oh! [*At Johnny's ear, jumping up and down*]

YELLOW: [*Stands out and talks to children.*] I just got a funny feeling. My Mommy and Daddy never tell me to take off my clothes when they read me a story.

SAFETY FRIEND: [*To Johnny*] Better say "no!" Better say "no!"

YELLOW: [*To children*] I think I'll say "no!" [*Turns back to babysitter*] No, I don't have to take my clothes off to hear a story.

PURPLE: It'll be okay, Johnny. I'll tell you what. I'll give you all the cookies you can eat if you take off your clothes.

SAFETY FRIEND: [*To Johnny, jumping up and down*] Uh-oh! Uh-oh!

YELLOW: [*Steps out and says to children*] I just got another funny feeling. My Mommy and Daddy don't give me cookies to take off my clothes.

SAFETY FRIEND: [*To Johnny*] Better say "no!" Better say "no!"

YELLOW: I'm going to say "no!" [*Turns back to babysitter*] No, I'm going to go into another room and play. I don't want to hear a story that way. [*To children as he walks away*] And when my mom and dad come home, I'm going to tell them what happened.

[*Review what the child did to keep safe when he got a funny feeling.*]

For 4- to 5-year-olds

PRESENTER 2: [*Without puppet*] What did Johnny do to keep himself safe when he got a funny feeling? [*Probe for: saying "no," not taking clothes off, not taking cookies, going elsewhere to play—walking away or keeping an arm's distance, and telling mom and dad.*]

For 2¹/₂- to 4-year-olds:

YELLOW (PRESENTER 2): I did a lot of things to keep myself safe when I got a funny feeling:

1. I said "no."

2. I didn't take my clothes off and let the babysitter touch me.

Concept: Keeping-safe skills

Note: *Ask older children directly. They may need to be prompted.*

Show Poster: *"What To Do."
Place poster between Purple
Puppet and Yellow Puppet.
Purple Puppet points to poster
while speaking.*

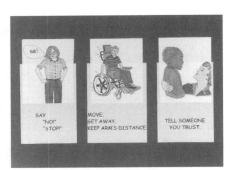

"WHAT TO DO" POSTER

Concept: *Saying "no!"*

Observer: *Lead applause after
each child says "no" and after
group "no"*

3. I didn't take the cookies.

4. I went into another room to play. I kept an arm's distance
and walked away.

5. And I'll tell my mom and dad when they get home.

ACTIVITY 4A

OBJECTIVES: By the end of Activities 4A and 4B, the children
will have learned to protect themselves by saying "no" and
using a safety yell.

We Can Say "No!"

PURPLE (PRESENTER 1): One thing Johnny did to keep himself safe was to say "no," just like this child is saying in the
poster. You can say "no" when someone wants you to touch
them in their private parts. We are all going to practice saying
"no" real loud and strong, but first Yellow Puppet will have a
turn.

PURPLE: [*Turns to Yellow Puppet*] Yellow Puppet, if I wanted to
touch you in your private parts or asked you to touch me in my
private parts, what would you say?

YELLOW (PRESENTER 2): [*Turns to Purple Puppet*] I would say
"no!"

PURPLE: Now everyone will get a chance to say "no" real loud
and strong.

YELLOW: [*To first child, starting with more responsive children, to
model for shyer ones.*] Can you stand up with me, hold my
hand, look Purple Puppet in the eye, and say "no" real loud and
strong? [*To next child*] What could you say if Purple Puppet
wanted to touch you in your private parts? Say "no" loud and
strong. [*To next child*] Could you say "no" if Purple Puppet
wanted you to touch her in her private parts?

[*Children stand up one at a time with Yellow Puppet (holding puppet's hand, if they like) and say "no" to Purple Puppet. No child
should be forced to stand up by himself or herself. He or she can
say "no" while sitting down. If a child doesn't want a turn, go on to*

the next child. Go around the room until each child has had a chance. After each child has had a turn, the whole group can say "no" together.]

PRESENTER 1: Everyone stand up and at the count of three let's all say "no" loud and strong to Purple Puppet. If Purple Puppet wanted to touch you in your private parts or wanted you to touch her, what could you say? **One, two, three... "NO!"**

ACTIVITY 4B

Safety Yell

PRESENTER 2: [*Without puppet*] Now we're going to teach you a special kind of yell. It's called the **"safety yell."** It's a yell that will help to keep you safe. It sounds like this: **UHHHHHHHH!** [*Demonstrate low-pitched yell from the diaphragm.*] That sounds different doesn't it? It's deep and low and loud. Now we're going to practice that yell together. Everyone stand up. [*This might be a good place to take a stretch break.*]

PRESENTER 2: Here's the special signal: when I count to three and raise my arm, we'll yell. When I put my arm down, we'll stop. Can you do that? Let's try now. One, two, three... [*Raise arm*]

GROUP YELL: UHHHHHHHH! [*No words, just sound; lower arm.*]

YELLOW (PRESENTER 2): [*When class has quieted down*] The safety yell is something you can do if you get a "no" or a "?" touch and you don't feel safe. You can also say "no!" real loud and strong. You can also keep an arm's distance. Now I can do a lot of things to keep myself safe and so can you!

ACTIVITY 5

OBJECTIVES: By the end of Activity 5, the children will have learned to use their safe-keeping skills in recognizing and protecting themselves from unwanted touch by people they know well.

Note: *Group "no" is optional. It is done when several children refuse to say "no" by themselves.*

Teach: *Safety Yell*

EARLY CHILDHOOD CURRICULUM **5**

Note: Place puppets on two chairs next to each other. Presenters kneel next to chairs on either side, with inside hand in puppet. Presenters show emotions on their faces.

Introduction

PRESENTER 1: [*Without puppets*] Sometimes people who touch children in their private parts, when the child doesn't like it or it makes the child feel funny, can be people the child knows. They can even be someone in the child's family, like an uncle or an aunt, a cousin, an older brother, or even a mother or father.

Father-Daughter Skit

YELLOW PUPPET (PRESENTER 2): We're going to do a play now about a little girl whose daddy touches her in her private parts. I'm going to be the little girl. I'm ___ years old. Mommy went to work tonight. Daddy and I are home alone together and I'm watching TV. **Purple Puppet is my daddy.** Let's see what happens.

DAD: Hi, honey! [*Sitting down next to daughter with arm around her*]

GIRL: Hi, Daddy!

DAD: Let's turn off the TV. I have a special game to teach you.

GIRL: [*Enthusiastically turns off TV*] What's the new game?

DAD: It's called the love game. You play it like this . . . [*He puts her hand on his leg and his hand on her leg.*] You put your hand here and I put my hand there. Isn't that nice?

[*Girl/Yellow Puppet looks uncomfortable, frowns, and fidgets. Girl/Yellow Puppet alternates between looking sad (by looking down and squirming) and looking pleased when Dad offers bribe.*]

DAD: If you play this game with Daddy, I'll buy you a cuddly new teddy bear.

GIRL: Well, okay. A new teddy bear? [*Looks sad and confused.*]

DAD: And remember, I want you to promise never to tell anybody about this game. **It's our secret.** Don't even tell Mommy.

GIRL: [*Looks confused*] I can't even tell Mommy?

DAD: No! You want that teddy bear don't you?

GIRL: [*Reluctantly*] Yes.

DAD: Okay. Then we'll play this love game and it will be our secret. [*Freeze action with Purple Puppet over Yellow Puppet. Emphasize Yellow Puppet's sad expression.*]

PRESENTER 1: Do you think Yellow Puppet likes this touch? Does she look sad? What kind of a touch do you think that was? Let's ask her and find out. [*Without puppet*] Did you like that touch Yellow Puppet?

Show: Touch signs in order (heart, no, ?)

YELLOW: No, I didn't like that touch. I didn't feel safe. I wanted it to stop.

PRESENTER 1: Then that was a "no" touch for you. Maybe that was a "?" touch, too.

YELLOW: Yes. I love my daddy, but I didn't like the way he was touching me all over and in my private parts.

PRESENTER 1: You may like the person, but you may not always like the touch. Maybe Yellow Puppet had a **funny feeling.** Remember when the daddy said, "Don't tell anyone about this game?" That was a **secret.** There are two kinds of secrets. One's like a surprise that you keep for a little while, and after you tell, everyone has a good time. When someone says: "Don't tell anyone ever!" when they touch you in your private parts, or want you to touch them, you can tell someone. **You don't have to keep this kind of a secret.**

Concept: Secret

PRESENTER 1: Is it the little girl's fault if she can't stop her daddy from touching her? No, **it's never the child's fault.** Whose fault is it? This time it's the daddy's fault. What can the little girl do to keep safe? Can she tell someone she trusts? Who can she tell? [*Get answers from children; one will say "Mommy".*] Yes, she can tell Mommy, even though her daddy said not to.

Concept: Never the child's fault

Mother-Daughter Skit
(Believing Mother—For Ages 3 to 5)

PRESENTER 2: In this next play the little girl tells her mommy. **Yellow Puppet** will be the little girl and **Green Puppet** will be the mommy. Watch and see what happens.

GIRL: Mommy, I didn't get to watch TV last night.

MOM: Why not, sweetie?

GIRL: Because Daddy wanted to play a game. He wanted to touch me down there. [*Points to crotch*] And he told me not to tell you.

MOM: Well, I'm glad you're telling me. Daddy shouldn't touch you there. That touching has to stop.

GIRL: I don't want to play that game anymore, Mommy.

MOM: You won't have to play that game anymore. I'm going to keep you safe. And you know what? It is not your fault. You're still the same wonderful little girl you were before. [*Puts arm around daughter and smiles. Freeze action and ask*]

PRESENTER 2: What kind of touch is this for the little girl? A "heart" touch! It's a touch that both people like and both people want. You know, sometimes the first person a child tells doesn't believe him or her. That's why it's important to tell, and tell, and tell, until someone does believe you. Who could you tell if someone was touching you in your private parts and you didn't like it or it made you feel funny?

[*Go around the semicircle and ask each child. Probe for other adults besides Mommy and Daddy.*]

Unbelieving Mother—For Oldest Children

PRESENTER 2: In this next play the little girl tells her mommy. Yellow Puppet will be the little girl and Green Puppet will be the mommy. Watch and see what happens.

GIRL: Mommy, I didn't get to watch TV last night.

Concept: Older people may not believe the child; tell someone else.

Note: For ages 3 to 5, use believing mother skit.

MOM: Why not, sweetie?

GIRL: Because Daddy wanted to play a game. He wanted to touch me down there. [*Points to crotch.*] And he told me not to tell.

MOM: Oh, don't be silly! Your daddy wouldn't do something like that. You must be mixed up. Now run along and play.

Concept: Older people may not believe the child.

YELLOW (PRESENTER 2): Sometimes people don't believe children when they try to talk about touching in private parts. My mommy didn't believe me. One of the things I could do is to **tell someone else.** Who else could I tell? [*Neighbors, grandparents, aunt, uncle, etc.*] Or you can try to **tell the same person again.** That's what I did. Let's see what happens this time.

Concept: Tell someone else or tell the same person again.

Redo Mother-Daughter Skit with Positive Outcome—For Oldest Children

GIRL: Mommy, I didn't get to watch TV last night.

MOM: Really?

GIRL: Yes. Daddy wanted to play that Love Game again and he touched me in my private parts and made me promise not to tell you.

MOM: [*Looking concerned*] Well, I'm glad you're telling me. You know, at first I didn't believe you. But if you're telling me again, it must be so.

GIRL: I don't like the game, Mommy. Do I have to play?

MOM: No, honey. I'm glad you told me because that touching has to stop. Your daddy shouldn't touch you there. I'm going to keep you safe. And you know what? It is not your fault. You're still the same wonderful little girl you were before. [*Puts arm around daughter and smiles.*]

PRESENTER 2: What kind of touch is this for the little girl? A "heart" touch! This little girl told her mommy again, and she got help. Who else can she tell? Who could you tell? Who do you trust?

Note: If children's attention span is limited, omit the question, "Who else can you tell?" here. It will be covered in the review.

[*Ask each child to name someone. Go around the semicircle. Probe for other adults besides Mommy and Daddy. Grandma or Grandpa? Auntie? Uncle? Teacher?*]

Stretch Break (*if needed*)

ACTIVITY 6

Optional For Older Children, Time Allowing

OBJECTIVE: By the end of Activity 6, children will have learned to identify and describe people, in case they need to do so after an incident.

Identification Game

Concept: *Identify strangers*

PRESENTER 1: [*Without puppets*] If someone you don't know touches you in your private parts or wants you to touch them in their private parts, you may have to tell someone you trust what that person looks like. Here's _____. [*Points to Observer. Observer stands in front of children while being described.*] **Let's try to describe him or her.** [*Skin color; eye color; hair color, length; body build; height; what the person is wearing; where did you see him or her? When did you see him or her?*]

ACTIVITY 7

Review

OBJECTIVE: To review the concepts learned in Activities 2 through 5 in Session 2

[*Yellow Puppet (Presenter 2) acts out each skill.*]

Note: *Review can be abbreviated, as in Day 1. Remember to stress saying "no," telling someone, pointing to the private parts, and that it's never the child's fault.*

PRESENTER 1: Let's remember all the things we talked about. There are many things you can do to keep safe when someone touches you in your private parts or wants you to touch them in their private parts. You can:

- Say "no." [*Yellow says "no!"*]

- Run away. [*Yellow runs away.*]

- Trust your funny feelings. [*Yellow says "Uh-oh, better say no!"*]

- Keep an arm's distance. [*Presenter 1 demonstrates with Yellow.*]

● Call for help/use safety yell. [*Yellow does yell.*]

● Tell someone you trust. [*Yellow says to Presenter 1:
"Mommy, someone is touching me and I don't like it."*]

YELLOW PUPPET (PRESENTER 2): Who can you tell?

● Mommy or Daddy

● Uncle or Aunt

● Big Brother or Sister

● Grandparents

● Teacher

● Neighbor

[*Have children come up to the Safety Friend picture, or stand and
point to their private parts.*]

PRESENTER 1 (SAFETY FRIEND): Here's Safety Friend. Let's
find the private parts on Safety Friend's picture. These are private parts on Safety Friend's body and on your body too. And
no one should touch you in your private parts, if you don't
like it, or if it makes you feel funny. [*Or have children stand up
together and all point to their private parts.*]

PRESENTER 1 (SAFETY FRIEND): If a child can't stop a touch,
is it the child's fault? No, **it's never the child's fault.** It's always
the fault of the bigger or older person who's touching the child.

PRESENTER 2: Remember the three kinds of touches? The
"heart" touch, "no" touch, and "?" touch. Let's all sing the first
part of "The Touching Song!" (See page 146 for the full lyrics of
"The Touching Song.")

"THE TOUCHING SONG" WITH SIGNS

Note: Always end with the chorus
of the song. Presenters and
Observer sing the chorus without
puppets. Each holds a touch sign.

ACTIVITY 8

Private Time

OBJECTIVE: Same as Session 1, Activity 6

PRESENTER 2: If anyone has anything he or she wants to tell
us or ask us in private, we'll be here again, like yesterday.

6

Elementary Curriculum

Session 1

ACTIVITY 1

OBJECTIVES: By the end of Activity 1, the children will have learned *Keeping Kids Safe* ground rules and definitions of "child abuse," with an emphasis on child sexual abuse.

Classroom Setup

In the classroom, or in a predesignated room (library, activity room, cafeteria) two Presenters and one Observer (optional) should set up an appropriate number of chairs in a semicircle for the children. Allow enough room behind the semicircle to enable the observer to move freely behind the class during the presentation. In a classroom setting, the children and teacher can help move tables, desks, and chairs. Prior to the class, the presenter should meet with the teacher to determine the number of children in the class and to find out if any children may need special attention. The teacher can also be helpful in determining which children should not sit together and which children may need translation services. Invite the teacher to sit in the circle with the children.

The Presenters will need to place two chairs in the front center of the semicircle, allowing for children on the ends to see adequately. Place presentation posters and signs behind these chairs for easy access. The observer should take out an Observer/Presentation form and begin to fill out the necessary information.

Introduction and Ground Rules

● [*Observer and Presenters put on children's name tags. Teachers, aides, visitors, and the team also get name tags.*]

● **PRESENTER 1:** [*Stand up. Introduce program, Self, Co-Presenter, Observer, and Visitors.*] We are from the *Keeping Kids Safe* program. We are going to be telling you some important information, but before we do, I want to go over our ground rules.

1. So that we can all hear each other, only one person can talk at a time. That means that when we are talking, you're listening, and when you're talking, we'll listen to you, because we really want to hear what you have to say.

2. If you have a question or an answer to one of our questions, please raise your hand. We call on quiet hands.

3. Some of the things we have to say may be embarrassing and may make you giggle. That's because hardly anyone ever talks about the things we're going to tell you. And it's okay to giggle. But we also want you to listen very carefully, because the things we have to tell you may help you keep safe.

4. You're sitting where you want to now. But if you talk to your neighbor, and make it hard for others to hear, we will have to move you.

5. We give you name tags so that we can call on you by name. Please leave your name tags on your shirts so that we can see them.

6. After today's and tomorrow's presentations, we'll be available to talk in (predesignated room) if you have a question about something you didn't understand or something you'd like to tell us by yourself, or privately. We call this time Private Time.

Notes: *Presenters can either sit or stand. Standing gives greater emphasis to the instructions. Shorten the rules depending on the feel of the class.*

Purpose: To define various forms of child abuse

Definition of Sexual Abuse

PRESENTER 2: Does anyone know why we are here? [*Take two or three answers.*] We are here to talk about child abuse. Most of the time, adults take care of the children around them. But when an adult hurts a child, that may be child abuse. **When a grownup hurts a child so much that it leaves a mark or a bruise, that's child abuse.** It's more than a spanking. Sometimes kids are abused without being touched at all. When kids don't get the food, or clothing, or even the love they need, that's abuse too! And, other times, the hurt can't even be seen. Like when a grownup keeps calling a child names so much that the child starts to believe they can't do anything right. This is another kind of abuse that hurts on the inside. Today and tomorrow we're going to talk about another kind of abuse called "child sexual abuse." **Sexual abuse is when someone tries to force or trick a child into touching private parts of their own body or another person's body.** The private parts are the mouth, the chest, between the legs, and the bottom. [*Presenters point to private parts.*] All of these things we are talking about are against the law. **That means that if anything like this is happening to you, it's important to tell someone to get help to stop the abuse.**

ACTIVITY 2

OBJECTIVES: By the end of Activity 2, the children will have learned about the concept of personal body safety and three body safety rights.

Body Safety Rights

Purpose: To define concept of rights and establish that kids have rights

Concept: Body Safety Rights

PRESENTER 1: We are here to talk with you about different ways you can keep yourself safe from forced or tricked touch. But first, do you think you have any rights? **Rights are things you can do just because you're alive.** What rights do children have? Do you have the right to sleep? To eat? To have fun? To get a good education? These are all rights that we have just because we're alive. How would you feel if someone came into this class and said, "For the rest of this week this class can't have recess." If they took your right to have recess away, how would you feel inside? [*Take three answers.*]

Well, we want to tell you about three body safety rights you have, that everyone has. And if someone took these special rights away from you, you might also feel [*Use their responses*] sad, mad, like it wasn't fair.

Your special body safety rights are:

1. The right to feel safe from forced or tricked touch.

2. The right to ask questions about forced or tricked touch to private parts of your body or the other person's body.

3. And the right to say "no" to forced or tricked touch. If someone forces or tricks you into touch, you can say "no!"

Feeling Safe

PRESENTER 1: One of your body safety rights is the right to feel safe. How do you feel inside when you're safe? [*Take three answers.*]

There are many different ways to feel safe. Look at this poster. All of these kids feel safe in different ways. Some kids feel safe with their families. Some kids feel safe when they are with a group of friends, or with one special friend. These kids feel safe with their pet. This girl feels safe when she's playing with her toy. This girl feels safe when she's all by herself. Some kids think if their rights are taken away, it's their fault. Is it the child's fault if she or he can't stop the forced or tricked touch?

No, it's never the child's fault. It's always the fault of the older or bigger person who took the child's body safety rights away.

ACTIVITY 3

OBJECTIVES: By the end of Activity 3, the children will have learned to differentiate among touches and will learn at least three safe-keeping strategies.

Touch Continuum

Introduction to Touches

PRESENTER 2: Now we want to tell you about three kinds of touches.

1. A "heart" touch feels good and both people like and want it. [*Show sign.*]

Show Poster: *"Special Body Rights." Presenter 2 helps Presenter 1 hold poster, making sure it is visible to all.*

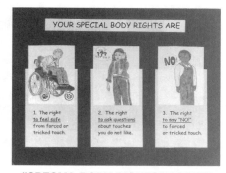

"SPECIAL BODY RIGHTS" POSTER

Show Poster: *"Safe Scenes." Presenter 2 helps to hold on one side while Presenter 1 points.*

"SAFE SCENES" POSTER

Concept: *Never the child's fault*

Concept: *Kinds of touches*

Note: *Show touch signs*

Purpose: *To teach kids to differentiate between comfortable, uncomfortable, and confusing touches*

"THE TOUCHING SONG" WITH SIGNS

Note: Presenter 1 sets up touch plays. Presenter 2 leads touch votes. Make sure both Presenters face audience during plays. Accentuate facial expressions. Stand back far enough so that entire class can see.

2. A "no" touch feels bad. You don't like it and want this kind of touch to stop. [*Show sign.*]

3. A "?" touch is a mixed-up, confusing kind of touch. You're not sure how you feel about this touch. Maybe you like the touch at first, but then you change your mind and don't like it anymore. Or maybe you like the person who's touching you, but don't like the touch. [*Show sign.*]

We are going to do some plays about this now. We will show you different kinds of touches and we want you to decide if you think they are "heart" touches, "no" touches, or "?" touches. [*Show signs again in order of mention.*] After we do each play, we'll take a vote. Remember that when we vote, there are all kinds of answers. Everyone has a different idea. You can even vote more than once.

Touch Plays/Votes

[Identify who is playing which role. Identify sex and age of players. Make younger child's age same as ages of children in classroom. Presenters should alternate victim and offender roles, to avoid typecasting.

Discourage calling out by saying, "Raise your hand if. . . ." Children with different answers may hold them back if peers call out "yes" or "no" during vote. Get two answers for each vote when possible.

After each child's answer say "uh-huh" or "okay"; then repeat answer for all to hear. Make sure to support each answer, not judge it. Show correct sign last each time. If most popular answer is shown first, children may not vote for other answers.]

Tickle Touch

PRESENTER 1: In this play, _____ (Presenter 2) is going to be my younger sister. She's ___ (same age as children in class) years old. I'm her older sister and I'm ___ (several years older). We are playing at home. Watch and see what happens.

PRESENTER 1: Hi _____ (Presenter 2's name)!

PRESENTER 2: Hi _____ (Presenter 1's name)!

PRESENTER 1: Want to play a game?

PRESENTER 2: Sure! What kind of game?

PRESENTER 1: It's called the tickle game. Ready?

[*Presenter 1 tickles Presenter 2. Touch goes on too long. Presenter 2's expression changes from a smile to a frown. Presenter 2 moves away as Presenter 1 reaches out to continue tickling. Freeze action.*]

VOTE

PRESENTER 2: Remember that there are all kinds of answers. So, if you thought it was a "heart" touch, raise your hand. How could you tell? [*Two answers*] If you thought it was a "no" touch, raise your hand. How could you tell? [*Two answers*] If you thought that might have been a "?" touch also, raise your hand. How could you tell? [*Two answers*] Raise your hand if you like to be tickled. Raise your hand if you don't like to be tickled. You see, everyone has different feelings about touches, and you can make up your own mind about a touch.

Bully Touch

PRESENTER 1: In this next play, I'm going to be a boy in the ____ (same grade as children) grade. I'm waiting at the bus stop after school on my way home. ____ (Presenter 2) is an older kid in middle school that I don't know. Watch and see what kind of touch this is for me. [*Stands in front of children waiting, looking at watch, looking for bus, whistling or humming.*]

PRESENTER 2: Hey kid, move! Get Lost! That's my spot! [*Pushes Presenter 1 out of way. Looks mean.*]

[*Presenter 1 looks sad and angry. Moves off to the side. Presenter 2 stands with hands on hips, glaring at Presenter 1.*]

VOTE

PRESENTER 2: If you thought that was a "heart" touch, raise your hand. [*Most children won't vote for this.*] If you thought it was a "?" touch, raise your hand. How could you tell? [*Two answers*] If you thought that was a "no" touch, raise your hand. How could you tell? [*Two answers*] Do people like to be bullied and pushed around? No!

An Appropriate Hug

PRESENTER 1: You're doing really great! Let's see how you do on this one. This time I'm going to be _____'s (Presenter 2) Aunt Janie. I'm going to come to her house to visit. _____ (Presenter 2) is ___ (age of children) years old. Watch and see what happens. [*Walks from side to middle/front and knocks on imaginary door*] Knock! Knock! Knock!

PRESENTER 2: Who is it? [*Asks before opening*]

PRESENTER 1: It's your Aunt Janie!

PRESENTER 2: [*Looks through imaginary peephole*] Aunt Janie! [*As she opens door with a big smile on her face.*]

PRESENTER 1: [*Gives Presenter 2 big hug*] Good to see you!

[*Both presenters like and want this touch. They smile toward class as they hug each other so children can see their expressions.*]

VOTE

PRESENTER 2: If you thought that was a "no" touch, raise your hand. [*Some children may not like to be hugged, but most will not vote for this.*] If you thought it was a "?" touch, raise your hand. [*Two answers.*] How about a "heart" touch? How could you tell? [*Two answers.*] A "heart" touch is a touch both people like and want.

Surprise Touch (Entrapment)

PRESENTER 1: You're really catching on to this! Let's see what you think about this one. In this play we are best friends and we're both in the ___ (same as children) grade. I'm getting a drink of water at the water fountain at school. Watch and see what kind of touch this is for me.

[*Presenter 1 bends over to get a drink; facing kids. Presenter 2 silently tiptoes up behind Presenter 1. Encircles friend around the arms in a bear hug. Presenter 1 looks very startled and gasps. Shows surprised expression to all children. No words are spoken.*]

PRESENTER 2: If you thought that was a "heart" touch, raise your hand. Remember there are all kinds of answers. Different people feel differently about touches. [*Take two answers.*] Some children may feel this was a playful game between friends. If you thought that was a "no" touch, raise your hand. How could you tell? [*Two answers*] Does everyone like to be surprised that way? It's kind of like the tickle touch, huh? Did anybody think it was a "?" touch? Raise your hand and tell us how you could tell. [*Three answers. Emphasize that you may like your friend, but you may not like the way your friend touches you.*]

Father Hugging Son Good-bye

PRESENTER 1: In this play I'm going to be a boy and I'm ___ (same age as children) years old. I'm getting ready to go to school in the morning. _____ (Presenter 2) is my dad. Watch and see what kind of touch this is for me.

PRESENTER 2: Are you ready for school? Have you got your lunch?

PRESENTER 1: Uh-huh.

PRESENTER 2: Do you have your homework?

PRESENTER 1: Uh-huh. See you later, Dad! [*Gives Dad a hug.*]

PRESENTER 2: [*Hugs son.*] Bye-bye! Have a nice day! [*Both Presenters smile, showing class that both want and like touch.*]

VOTE

PRESENTER 2: If you thought that was a "?" touch, raise your hand. How could you tell? [*Three answers*] If you thought that was a "no" touch, raise your hand. [*Three answers*] If you thought that was a "heart" touch, raise your hand. How could you tell? [*Three answers*] Did it look like we both liked and wanted that touch? **A heart touch is a touch both people want and both people like.**

Note: *Bigger presenter may wish to play Uncle Sam*

Uncle Sam Touch (Uncomfortable for Child)

PRESENTER 1: Are you ready for the last play? In this one _____ (Presenter 2) is going to be a girl who's ____ (same age as kids) years old. I'm going to be her Uncle Sam. We are at a family get-together. We haven't seen each other in a long time. Watch and see what kind of touch this is for _____ (Presenter 2).

PRESENTER 2: Hi, Uncle Sam!

PRESENTER 1: Come sit on my lap! It's been such a long time since I've seen you!

PRESENTER 2: Okay! [*Sits on lap willingly and happily smiles at Uncle Sam.*]

PRESENTER 1: What a pretty girl you are! You're getting so big! I bet you have lots of boyfriends, huh! Gosh, it's great to have you here on my lap!

[*After Presenter 2 sits on Uncle Sam's lap, Presenter 1 begins to hug her tightly and rub and stroke her thigh. The touch becomes intrusive and tentatively sexual. Emphasis is on stroking the thigh. Presenter 2 squirms and looks uncomfortable and confused, but stays on Uncle Sam's lap. Freeze action.*]

VOTE

PRESENTER 2: If you thought that was a "heart" touch, raise your hand. If you thought that was a "no" touch, raise your hand. How could you tell? [*Three answers*] If you thought it was also a "?" touch, raise your hand. How could you tell? [*Three answers*] Did I want to sit on my uncle's lap at first? Then what happened? I changed my mind. Can you change your mind about a touch? You sure can. Is it possible to like my Uncle Sam but not like the touch? Yes, **we may really like the person, even though we may not like the touch.**

Concepts: *Never the child's fault. Tell someone you trust.*

PRESENTER 2: If a child can't stop a "no" or "?" touch, is it the child's fault? No, **it's never the child's fault.** Whose fault was it in this case? Yes, Uncle Sam's. The person who forced and tricked me into touching. And what can a child do afterward to make sure it doesn't happen again? Yes. **Tell someone you trust.**

Brainstorming Safety Skills

PRESENTER 1: You voted that some of these touches were "no" touches and some were "?" touches. What can a child do to keep safe in these situations? For example, if your big sister was tickling you and you wanted that touch to stop, what would you do? [*Three to five answers*] What if a big bully came up to you at the bus stop and tried to push you out of the way? Think of ways to get that touch to stop that use your brainpower. Remember, it's a much bigger and older kid. [*Three to five answers*]

PRESENTER 1: Here's something else you could do in this situation to keep safe. Let's say ___ (Presenter 2) is standing at the bus stop. Watch what he (or she) does this time to keep safe [*Presenter 1 tries to push Presenter 2, but this time Presenter 2 moves away, keeping an arm's distance or more away, so that Presenter 1 can't touch her or him.*] Can I push her or him? Can I grab her or him? No! Because he or she is keeping at least an arm's distance away. That's something you can do too. And that will give you extra time to turn and run for help.

PRESENTER 1: How about in the surprise touch? Remember when I was drinking water, and _____ (Presenter 2) crept up behind me to surprise me? If I didn't like that touch and wanted it to stop, what could I do to keep myself safe? [*Three to five answers. Explore who to tell.*] If I still couldn't get the touch to stop, who could I tell? What about in the last play we did? Remember when _____ (Presenter 2) was my niece and she didn't like it when her uncle was rubbing her leg? What could a child do to keep safe in that situation? [*Three to five answers*] And what could you do afterward to make sure it didn't happen again? Who could you tell? [*Three answers*]

PRESENTER 1: If a child can't stop a "no" or a "?" touch, is it the child's fault? No. Whose fault is it? It's always the fault of the person who's forcing or tricking the child into touch. What can a child do afterwards so it doesn't happen again? Tell someone he or she trusts. Remember, different things work for different people. You need to find the skills that work best for you.

Purpose: To teach children skills to use when confronted with "no" or "?" touches

Teach: Arm's distance technique

Note: In brainstorming section, emphasize saying "no," running or walking away, screaming or yelling for help, and telling someone you trust. If kids mention these themselves, repeat for class to hear. Otherwise, prompt them.

Concepts: Never the child's fault

Importance of telling

Different skills work for different people.

Purpose: *To give an opportunity for children to practice skills*

Note: *Be sure to alternate sex and ethnicity of children when picking helpers. No child should be forced to participate.*

Purpose: *Involve children who are more shy*

Class Participation/Practice of Safety Skills

[*Observer leads applause after each re-do.*]

PRESENTER 2: Now we're going to do the "question mark" and "no" plays again, and see how you could stop the touches using some of the ideas we've just talked about, or some other ideas you may have. We need your help.

Would someone like to come up and practice keeping safe from the tickle touch?

[*Presenter 2 picks a child to help. Takes child aside plans quietly what he or she will to keep safe. Plan must not include hitting, kicking, or taking away of presenter's body rights. Support child's ideas. Always ask child "Who would you tell?" even if child does not include this in role-play.*]

PRESENTER 1: [*While Presenter 2 plans role-play*] What would you do to keep safe if someone started tickling you and you didn't like it? [*Call on children who have not said much. Circulate around the room. Repeat answers to keep everyone's attention.*]

[*Re-do.*]

PRESENTER 1: Acts out skit with child. Tries to tickle child and stops tickling when child does something to keep safe.

[*All applaud*]

PRESENTER 2: [*When child has finished skit*] What did _____ do to keep safe? [*Three answers*] Good work! Now we need another helper to practice keeping safe from the bully touch.

PRESENTER 1: [*Brainstorms with class*] What if a big kid started bullying you and said, "If you tell anyone, I'll beat you up!" Who could you tell? [*Repeat above steps for this re-do, as well as for "surprise" and "uncle" touches.*] What if someone you like touches you in a way you don't like?

[*Redo Bully, Surprise, and Uncle Sam plays using the model given on this page.*]

PRESENTER 2: Now you know different things you can do to keep safe from "no" and "?" touches. You have many choices about how to stop a forced or confusing touch. You can say "no!" or "stop!" You can tell someone you trust, you can yell, you can run away, or keep an arm's distance. But remember, you need to find the way to keep safe that works best for you.

ACTIVITY 4

OBJECTIVES: By the end of Activity 4, the children will have learned a song that illustrates the three kinds of touches and reinforces safe-keeping strategies learned in Activity 3.

"The Touching Song"

PRESENTER 1: Now we're going to sing a song about the three kinds of touches. It's called "The Touching Song." You can sing the chorus with us if you'd like when you learn it. [*Call up Observer to sing with two Presenters. Each holds up one of the touch signs.*]

Chorus
There are three kinds of touches, this we know—
A "heart," a "question mark," and "no."
"No" means stop,
"Heart" means go,
"Question mark" means "I don't know."

Verse 1
Now, if I tickle you and you say "no"
And I don't stop, where should you go?
You could go and tell somebody you know
And keep very safe from the tickle-o.

Chorus: *There are three kinds of touches...*

Verse 2
What if a bully pushes you down
And there's nobody else around?
You can run for help because, you see,
That's a "no" touch, we all agree.

Chorus: *There are three kinds of touches...*

Purpose: *Introduce "The Touching Song"*

"THE TOUCHING SONG" WITH SIGNS

"THE TOUCHING SONG" — QUESTION MARK

Verse 3
You see Aunt Janie only once a year
And when she finally does appear,
She gives you a heart touch, that's very clear.
We can see you grin from ear to ear!

Chorus: There are three kinds of touches...

Verse 4
When you sit on his lap, your Uncle Sam
Is sweet and tender as a lamb.
But if "lamb-Sam" touches you where you don't like,
You can tell him to "go take a hike!"

Chorus: There are three kinds of touches...

ACTIVITY 5

OBJECTIVES: By the end of Activity 5, the children will have learned about other forms of sexual abuse that don't involve touch.

Other Kinds of Sexual Abuse/Harassment

PRESENTER 1: Today we've been talking about different kinds of touches that kids get. Tomorrow we'll be talking more about what kids can do if they get forced or tricked into touching private parts of the body. That's called "sexual abuse." Sometimes sexual abuse can be other things too, things that don't involve/ have anything to do with [*use second phrase with grades K through 2*] touching. Has anyone ever heard of:

A **Flasher?** Yes, a flasher is someone who opens up a coat or their pants to show their private parts. This is a type of sexual abuse that doesn't involve touching, but is against the law.

How about a **Peeping Tom?** A Peeping Tom is someone who sneaks peeks at people when they're dressing or undressing or bathing. This is a form of sexual abuse that doesn't involve touching, but is also against the law.

How many of you have heard of an **obscene phone call?** [*Take three answers.*] Yes, that's when someone calls on the phone and says things that make you feel uncomfortable. Or maybe they just breathe or don't say anything at all. That's another form of abuse that doesn't involve touching, but is also against the law. What is the first thing you can do to keep safe if you get an obscene phone call? **Hang up the phone and tell someone you trust about the call.**

All of these examples are forms of sexual abuse that don't involve touching, but are against the law.

ACTIVITY 6

OBJECTIVES: By the end of Activity 6, the children will have reviewed the basic concepts taught in Session 1.

Review

PRESENTER 1:

Purpose: To determine the extent of children's learning after Session 1

1. What is sexual abuse? [*Get two answers. If answers are not complete, say: Sexual abuse is when someone forces or tricks a child into touching private parts of their own body or the other person's body.*]

2. What are your three special body rights? Let's say them together: You have the right to feel safe. You have the right to ask questions. You have the right to say "no!" [*If necessary, pull out poster to remind them.*]

3. a. What can you do to keep yourself safe if you get a "no" or "?" touch? [*Emphasize saying "no!"; running; telling someone; keeping an arm's distance; yelling for help.*]

   b. Who could you tell? [*Mom, Dad, teacher, etc.; encourage kids to think of other resources.*]

4. If a child can't stop what's happening, is it the child's fault? [*No, it is never the child's fault. It is always the fault of the person forcing or tricking the child into touch.*]

5. And if a child can't stop what's happening, what can he or she do afterwards so that it doesn't happen again? [*Tell someone he or she trusts.*]

Purpose: To introduce Private Time

ACTIVITY 7

OBJECTIVES: To give children the opportunity to clear up confusion about touches and to get help in stopping unwanted touches

Private Time

PRESENTER 1: Tomorrow we'll be back again to talk to you about more things you can do to keep yourself safe. We will be here at the same time tomorrow. But, before we leave today, we're going to have Private Time. This is a time when you can talk to one of us by yourself. You can ask any questions or talk about something that's on your mind. If you have a question or something you'd like to share about touches, please raise your hand. [*Presenter 2 writes the names on the board or a piece of paper.*] **Thank you. You've been a great class!**

Session 2

. . . .

<u>ACTIVITY 1</u>

OBJECTIVES: By the end of Activity 1, the children will have reviewed the ground rules and main concepts of Session 1.

Setup, Introduction, and Ground Rules

- *[Set up the room in the same way as the day before.]*

- *[Observer and both Presenters put on children's name tags. Name tags are again given to teacher, aides, and visitors, and are worn by the team as well.]*

- *[Presenter 1 reintroduces* Keeping Kids Safe *program, Co-Presenter, Observer, and Visitors.]*

- *[Presenter 1 Reviews Ground Rules]*

  1. One person talks at a time

  2. Need to raise hands

  3. We will move children who disrupt class

  4. It's okay to giggle, but important to listen

- **PRESENTER 1:** We will have Private Time again today after our presentation. If you have questions or something you'd like to share, you can come see us by yourself when we're through.

Review

PRESENTER 2: Who remembers what sexual abuse is? [*Take two answers. Give our definition if children don't.*] What are your three Special Body Rights? Let's say them together. [*Show poster.*] What are some things you can do to keep yourself safe if you get a "no" or "?" touch? [*Three to five answers*] Who can you tell? [*Three to five answers*] If a child can't stop the forced or tricked touch, is it the child's fault? No. And what can a child do afterwards to make sure it doesn't happen again? Tell someone she or he trusts. You remember quite a lot from yesterday.

Purpose: *To reintroduce* Keeping Kids Safe *program and team*

Note: *Presenter 1 should keep track of length of presentation*

Purpose: *To review concepts taught in Session 1*

Show Poster: *"Special Body Rights"*

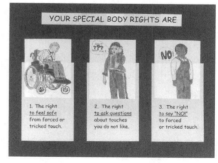

"SPECIAL BODY RIGHTS" POSTER

Show Poster: *"What To Do"*

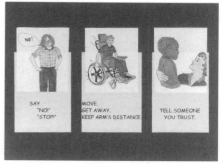

"WHAT TO DO" POSTER

Show Poster: *"Where It Can Happen"*

"WHERE IT CAN HAPPEN" POSTER

Purpose: *To demystify sexual abuse and give correct information*

Show Poster: *"When It Can Happen"*

"WHEN IT CAN HAPPEN" POSTER

Remember: *Avoid saying "right" or "wrong" after a child's answer. Instead, repeat the answer, then propose an alternate when appropriate.*

Emphasize: *Universality (anywhere, any time, any adult, any child)*

Show Poster: *"Potential Offenders"*

"POTENTIAL OFFENDERS" POSTER

ACTIVITY 2

OBJECTIVES: By the end of Activity 2, the children will have learned that sexual abuse can happen anywhere and anytime, that anyone can force or trick them into touch, and that any child is vulnerable to sexual abuse.

Myths and Facts about Sexual Abuse

PRESENTER 2: Where do you think sexual abuse happens? In what kinds of places can children get forced or tricked into touch? [*Take three to five answers. Show "Where It Can Happen" poster. Then both Presenters hold poster while Presenter 2 points. In large classes one presenter can walk around with the poster, so that the entire class can see.*] Can it happen in a park? Can it happen in a store? A video arcade? A car? Can children be forced or tricked into someone's house? Yes. Children can be sexually abused—forced or tricked into touching private parts of their own body or the other person's body—anywhere. It can happen anywhere.

When do you think sexual abuse happens? What time of the day or night are children forced or tricked into touching private parts of the body? [*Take three to five answers. Show "When It Can Happen" poster. Both Presenters hold poster while Presenter 2 points to different times of the day, going around the clock.*]

Can it happen in the middle of the night when a child's in bed? Can it happen in the morning when a child is getting ready to go out? Can a child be forced or tricked into touching in the middle of the day? How about in the afternoon, while walking home from school? Before or after a meal? Can it happen when a child's getting ready for bed?

Sexual abuse, or forced or tricked touch, can happen any time of the day or night.

What kinds of people sexually abuse children? [*Take three to five answers.*] If children say "drunks," "crazies," "gays," or "drug addicts," say "maybe," and ask if it could be the opposite kind of person. For example, "people who never drink or take drugs." [*Show "Potential Offenders" poster.*]

Can men sexually abuse kids? Can women force or trick children into touch? How about older people? Young people? People who look like this? People who wear suits? Uniforms?

There are two kinds of people who sexually abuse children: strangers and people you know. Most of the time it is someone the child knows. You can't tell by looking at someone. **Anyone can force or trick kids into touching private parts of their body or the child's body.**

Who do you think can be sexually abused? What kinds of kids get forced or tricked into touching private parts of their own body or the other person's body? [*Take three to five answers. Show "Any Kind of Child" poster.*]

Can boys be sexually abused? Can it happen to girls? Big kids? Little kids? Babies? Kids in the ___ (grade of class) grade? Kids who look like this?

Sexual abuse happens to both boys and girls. All kinds of children can be forced or tricked into touch. If a child can't stop the forced or tricked touch, is it the child's fault? **No, it is never the child's fault.** It's always the fault of the bigger or older person who's forcing or tricking the child into touching.

And if you can't stop the forced or tricked touch, you can tell someone afterwards, so that you can get the touching to stop.

Show Poster: "Any Kind of Child"

"ANY KIND OF CHILD" POSTER

ACTIVITY 3

OBJECTIVES: By the end of Activity 3, the children will have learned about intuition and how to employ their funny feelings to keep themselves safe.

Funny Feelings

Introduction

PRESENTER 1: Yesterday we talked about ways kids can keep themselves safe from "no" or "?" touches. Today, we're going to talk about how kids can protect themselves from forced or tricked touches to private parts of their body. One tool you can use to protect yourself is something you probably already know about. We call it a "funny feeling." Funny feelings are kind of hard to describe, because everyone's funny feelings are different. **A funny feeling is something inside you. It may be like a little voice that tells you something's not okay. The little voice is like a warning, saying "Uh-oh! Better say 'no!'"**

Here's an example of a funny feeling I had.

Concept: Funny Feelings

Purpose: To define "intuition" and introduce it as another safe-keeping skill

a. One day I got on the bus, and the person sitting across from me was staring at me and I didn't feel safe. It wasn't the way they were dressed, but how they were looking at me that gave me the funny feeling. You know what I did to keep safe? I moved to the front of the bus by the bus driver.

(*Optional*)

b. One day I was walking home alone and had a funny feeling that I was being followed, but I didn't pay attention to my funny feelings. And then that voice inside me said "uh-oh!" again. And when I turned around to check my funny feeling, sure enough, there was someone behind me. [*Walk into circle while talking and then demonstrate turning around to look at other Presenter.*] I ran into the nearest store to be safe!

Has anyone in this room ever had a funny feeling? I thought you might. Has anybody had a funny feeling that you used to keep yourself safe? Would you like to tell us about it? [*Pick one child to share his or her funny feelings. Probe for how he or she kept safe. Repeat his or her answer.*] Even though it's hard to talk about these funny feelings, we think they're real. And you can use these funny feelings to keep yourself safe. **If you get a funny feeling about somebody, trust it.**

Stranger Role-Play

PRESENTER 1: Now we're going to do a play about a boy who got a funny feeling from someone he met outside of school one day. I'm going to be a boy named Johnny. I'm ___ (same age as children) years old. This [*points to Presenter 2*] is going to be a man I meet in the playground as I'm walking home. Watch and see if you can find the funny feelings.

BOY: [*Walks across the front of the room whistling or humming.*]

MAN: [*Approaches boy, gets close*] Hi there! How're you doin'? Hey, what's your name again? Uh...Uh... [*Snaps his fingers to trick boy into telling, pretending he forgot.*]

BOY: Johnny.

MAN: That's right! Johnny! My name's Mr. Jones. Say, I've seen you around here before. You go to that school over there, don't you?

BOY: Yeah, that's my school.

Purpose: To encourage children to think of how their intuition has kept them safe

Purpose: To illustrate the concept of funny feelings

Presenter 1 = boy

Presenter 2 = man

MAN: Well, I'm the new yard teacher.

BOY: Wait a minute. You're not the yard teacher. Mr. Garcia's (Lee's, Smith's) the yard teacher.

MAN: [*Hesitates*] Well, uh...he went back east for a couple of months. His mother is sick.

BOY: [*Scratching his head*] Oh.

MAN: Well, anyway, you're pretty strong-looking. You play any sports, Johnny? [*Feels boy's muscle*]

BOY: [*Beaming*] Yeah. I play softball (basketball, kickball, soccer).

MAN: You know, I might be able to get you on the softball team at school, now that I'm the yard teacher. You can be my star player. How would you like that?

BOY: [*Excitedly*] Great! I was never a star before. [*Smiles and looks proud*]

MAN: Say, listen Johnny. Now that we're getting to be such good friends, I wonder if you'd be able to do me a favor. I need to move these boxes over here [*Points down*] across the street. [*Points out*] Can you help me out? It'll only take a few minutes.

BOY: [*Hesitates, looks doubtful*] Uh, I don't know. My mom says I should go right home after school.

MAN: Aw, c'mon! I could really use the help of a big, strong guy like you!

BOY: No, I don't think so. [*Starts to walk away*]

MAN: Listen, I'll give you ten dollars if you help me. Nobody will ever know you've got it.

BOY: [*Coming closer when bribe is offered. Face expresses internal conflict.*] It's all for me?

MAN: Yeah, I promise. You just pick up that box and I'll get the one behind it!

Note: *Real yard teacher's name can be changed to suit the locality or ethnicity of children*

Purpose: *To help children identify the funny feelings*

Concepts:

1. bribes

   a. be on a team

   b. money

2. flattery

3. tricking boy to tell his name

4. pretending to be the yard teacher

5. boy knew he had to go right home after school

Note: *When someone mentions the ten dollars, ask what that's called. If no one mentions the ten dollars, prompt them and then ask them to define "bribe."*

BOY: Okay.

[*Boy reaches down for box. Man stands close behind him and grabs him around the arms, encircling boy's upper body. Freeze action. Show Boy's shocked face to entire class by moving upper body from one side of class to the other.*]

Brainstorming with Class

PRESENTER 2: Although we pretended, something like this really did happen to a boy in _____ (your locale). The boy was sexually abused—forced and tricked into touching private parts of his own body and the man's body.

Identifying Funny Feelings

PRESENTER 2:

1. Do you think Johnny had any funny feelings?

2. When did he get the funny feelings? [*Three answers. If children don't mention the following funny feelings, ask:*]

3. Did Johnny have a funny feeling when the man said he was the new yard teacher? Did Johnny know someone else as the yard teacher?

4. Did Johnny have a funny feeling when the yard teacher told him he could be on his team? Had this man ever seen Johnny play? Sometimes a person will flatter or say nice things about a child in order to trick him or her into touching. This man talked about making Johnny the star of his team without ever seeing him play.

5. How about when the man offered Johnny ten dollars to move the boxes—did Johnny have a funny feeling then? That's a lot of money just to move some boxes, isn't it?

6. What do we call it when someone offers to give you something—like ten dollars—to trick you into doing something for them? [*One answer*] It's a kind of a trick we call a "bribe." That's something else someone can use to trick a child into touching.

7. What else can people bribe kids with in order to force or trick them into touch? [*Three answers: mention candy, toys, ride in car, if kids don't.*]

8. What about at the very beginning of the play—did Johnny have a funny feeling when he first met the man? Remember the man snapped his fingers and tricked Johnny. What did he say? [One answer] He tricked Johnny into telling his name. Did he really know it?

9. Did Johnny say he had to go right home after school? Maybe that was another funny feeling. Did Johnny pay attention to that funny feeling? No, he didn't.

Redo Stranger Skit

PRESENTER 1: Now we're going to do this play again. But this time when I get any funny feelings, I'll tell you, and will you tell me how to keep myself safe?

[Boy walks across front of room, on his way home.]

MAN: Hi there! How're you doing? Hey, what's your name again? Uh...uh... [Snaps his fingers]

BOY: [To children] Uh-oh, I just got a funny feeling! Does this man know my name? Is he trying to trick me into telling him my name? Should I tell him? Do you have to tell strangers your name? Not if you don't feel safe. [To man] I don't know you!

MAN: Oh, that's okay. My name is Mr. Jones and I am the new yard teacher at that school over there. You go to that school, don't you?

BOY: [Shrugs shoulders. To children] Uh-oh, I just got another funny feeling. I've never seen this man before! Do you think he is the new yard teacher? Is he trying to trick me? Should I believe him? [To man] I don't know you!

MAN: Well, you're pretty strong-looking. You play any sports kid? [Tries to feel Johnny's muscles]

BOY: [Moves away and keeps an arm's distance away. To children] I am going to keep an arm's distance away from this person.

MAN: [Halts when boy does this.] You know, I am getting a few teams together, now that I am the yard teacher, and you can be the star on one of my teams!

Notes:

In re-do, boy speaks to children directly when identifying funny feelings.

When asking class questions, wait for their responses.

Then turn back to man to respond, using the safe-keeping skills students have suggested.

BOY: [*To children*] Uh-oh. I just got a funny feeling. This man has never seen me play. Is he trying to trick me? Is he trying to bribe me? What should I say? [*To man*] No thanks!

MAN: Say, listen kid, I wonder if you'd be able to do me a favor. See them boxes over here? [*Points*] I need to move these across the street and could really use the help of a big strong guy like you. Can you help me out?

BOY: No, my mom says I've got to go right home after school. [*Walks away*]

MAN: Hey, it'll only take a minute. I've got ten dollars for you if you'll help me. Nobody'll ever know you've got it.

BOY: [*To children*] Oh-oh. I've got another funny feeling. He says he'll give me ten dollars to just move some boxes across the street. Do you think he's trying to bribe me? What should I say? [*To man*] No thanks! [*To children*] I'm going into school to find out who this guy really is. [*Walks away*]

Keeping Safe Ideas

PRESENTER 2:

Purpose: To elicit creative keep-safe ideas from children

a. What did Johnny do to keep himself safe when he got those funny feelings? [*Three to five answers; reinforce saying "no," keeping an arm's distance, and all of the other skills Johnny used to keep himself safe.*]

Concept: Tell someone you trust

b. What could he have done after he got grabbed? [*Reinforce telling somebody he trusts*] Sometimes kids can't stop forced or tricked touch. Sometimes even adults can't. But you can always tell someone afterwards to make sure it doesn't happen again.

c. Who could Johnny tell? At school? At home? [*Three to five answers*]

ACTIVITY 4

Purpose: Introduce a deep, low, loud self-defense yell for help, from the diaphragm, that adults will take seriously.

OBJECTIVES: By the end of Activity 4, the children will have learned to protect themselves in dangerous situations by using a self-defense yell to call for help.

Teach Self-Defense Yell

PRESENTER 1: Here's something else Johnny could have used to keep himself safe after he got grabbed. We're going to show you **a special self-defense yell**—a yell that sounds different than other yells kids make. We think if a grownup hears this yell, they'll wonder what's wrong and come and help a child.

Usually when kids are playing in the playground, they yell from their throats, like this. [*Demonstrate high-pitched yell.*] When adults hear that, they think, "Oh, that's just kids playing." The self-defense yell is different because it comes from deep in your stomach. [*For older children say "It comes from the diaphragm." Indicate the diaphragm on yourself.*] The yell is deep, low, and loud and sounds like this: Uhhhhh! [*Demonstrate diaphragm yell.*] You can make this yell even when you're running away.

Now I'd like you all to stand up and get ready for this yell. Let's take a stretch and some deep breaths. Put your hand on your stomach and feel where the breath comes from.

Now we're going to practice this yell together on a special signal. I'm going to put my hand up and count to three. When I put my hand down, we'll all do a deep, low, and loud yell. When I put it back up, we'll stop and be completely quiet. Can you do that? Okay. One . . . two . . . three . . . Uhhhhh!

[*Applaud their yell.*] **What a great yell!** [*Pause until class settles down and is ready to listen again.*]

PRESENTER 1: Now I have a very important question to ask you. If Johnny had a funny feeling but didn't pay attention to it, is it his fault he got sexually abused? [*Pause*] **No, it's never the child's fault, even if the child didn't pay attention to his funny feelings.** And if Johnny couldn't stop the man from grabbing and sexually abusing him, is it his fault then? [*Pause for answers.*] Even if Johnny took the bribe, would it be his fault? It's **never** the child's fault. It's always the fault of the older person doing the touching. In this case, whose fault was it? [*Get answers.*] That's correct. It was the fault of the man pretending to be the yard teacher.

Concept: Never the child's fault.

PRESENTER 1: Let's go over all the things you can do to keep yourself safe: run away; walk away; call for your friends; keep an arm's distance; tell someone you trust; use the self-defense yell. **But remember, you need to do whatever works for you. No one way works for everyone. Different things work for different people.**

Purpose: Review and practice safety skills

Concept: Different skills work for different people

RE-DOS WITH CHILDREN

First Re-do with Children

PRESENTER 1: Now we're going to do this play again. This time we'll need your help. Who would like to come up and keep themselves safe this time? Let's have someone who didn't help yesterday, to give others a turn. [*Presenter 1 asks observer or Presenter 2 to read names of children who helped on Day 1 from class form.*]

Note: *Be sure to alternate the sex and ethnicity of children when picking helpers.*

1. **PRESENTER 1:** [*Picks a child to help. As in Session 1, takes child aside and plans what he or she will do to keep safe in Stranger Skit. Prompts child.*] **Are you going to tell your name? Are you going to keep an arm's distance?** [*And so on. Also asks who child could tell.*]

2. **PRESENTER 2:** [*Asks rest of class*] **What would you do if a stranger came up to you on the playground and said, "What's your name?" What if he tried to feel your muscles? Asked you to be on his team? Offered you ten dollars to move some boxes?** [*Take several answers for each question from entire class, circulating around the room to keep everyone's attention. Try to call on some of the shyer children who aren't participating, but never pressure a child for an answer. Also, call on children who seem disappointed they weren't picked.*]

Observer: *Clap after each child role-plays*

[*Presenter 2 plays the yard teacher and will need to improvise with the child. Be sure to ask child's name and try to feel child's muscle—but stop when child keeps an arm's distance. Ask if child goes to that school and would like to be on one of your teams. Then ask if child will help to move boxes. Offer a bribe if the child doesn't leave at first. When child finishes, cut action. Some children may go up to the teacher and tell. Give them a chance to do this. Some may not say anything. Keep saying your lines until they do something to keep safe. Presenter 1 will be there to prompt kids who freeze. Some may walk away at the beginning. Cut there and clap. Observer or Presenter 1 will lead applause.*]

After Role-Play

PRESENTER 2: What did _____ do to keep safe? [*Three to five answers*]

Second Re-do with Children

PRESENTER 1: Now we're going to do this play once more. This time we have a special plan. We need three helpers. Raise your hand if you'd like a turn and haven't helped yet.

[Presenter 1 picks three children and takes them aside to plan. Ask one child (boy or girl) to be the kid on the way home from school. As in first re-do, go over all the ways he or she can keep safe. When man asks child to move boxes, ask child to call for friends, either by name or with self-defense yell, or: "Hey, you guys!" Instruct the other children to play on the playground with you. Say you'll be playing frisbee or catch in the corner. When friend calls, have children say, "Leave our friend alone," then make their yell and run away. Presenter 2 brainstorms with rest of class while Presenter 1 and helpers plan re-do.]

Note: *The presenters should try to pick a mixed-sex group.*

PRESENTER 2:

1. What if you're waiting to be picked up from school and a woman you don't know drives up? She says she's a friend of your mom's and was sent to pick you up because your mom's sick in the hospital. She says she's supposed to drive you there. What would you do? [*Take two to three answers.*]

2. What if your babysitter [*For 4th and 5th graders you may want to say "older neighbor" or "friend who was watching you".*] said you could stay up real late, eat a bunch of cookies, and watch TV if you took off all your clothes and let him take pictures of you naked? [*Two to three answers*]

3. What if the teen-aged boy down the street was wrestling with you and put his hand up your dress or down your pants, and told you not to tell anyone or he'd beat you up? [*Two to three answers*]

Purpose: *"What If" Game*

Notes:

You may not get to all three "What If"s.

Try to call on children who haven't spoken up.

Stop brainstorming when helpers are ready.

Purpose: *To teach children the concept of strength in numbers rather than in size or physical strength*

Note: *Presenters may choose to omit this section, if pressed for time.*

[*Presenter 2 plays a stranger with one child; others play on the side with Presenter 1. Do role-play as before. Ask child to move boxes. Child will (hopefully!) call friends. Friends will ask questions, helping to keep child safe. When kids say, "Leave our friend alone" and do self-defense yell, Presenter 2 slinks off. Cut action. Applaud children's efforts.*]

PRESENTER 2: What did _____ do this time to keep safe? [*Three to five answers*] What did his or her friends do? [*Two to three answers*] So now you know you can keep yourself and your friends safe from forced or tricked touch.

ACTIVITY 5

OBJECTIVES: By the end of Activity 5, the children will have learned how to identify and describe people who try to force or trick them into touch. They will have become familiarized with the reporting process.

Reporting/Identification Game

PRESENTER 1: Sexual abuse, or forced or tricked touch, by strangers or people you know, is against the law. It's always important to tell someone about it, so the sexual abuse can stop. In order to find the stranger who forced or tricked you into touch, you will have to tell someone—the police or a social worker—what that person looks like. Even when it's someone you know, you will have to tell someone to get the touch to stop.

Now we're going to play a game to learn how to describe someone. Everyone take a good look at _____ (Presenter 2). Remember what she's wearing; how short or tall she is; what color eyes, hair, and skin she has. Now, everyone close their eyes, and if you can describe something about how _____ (Presenter 2) looks, raise your hand. Don't forget to keep your eyes closed.

[*Presenter 2 writes description on blackboard.*]

[*Presenters 1 and 2: Try to avoid the children's judgmental or subjective descriptions by rephrasing them and turning them into comparisons. This is especially useful for comparisons of height and weight. Ask: Is he or she taller than me? Shorter than me? Is he or she white? Black? Prompt for: marks on skin; hair color, length, and style; eye color; clothing; jewelry; age (teenager's age, mother's age, grandmother's age); etc.]*

You may also need to report where it happened. Where are we now? And you might have to report when it happened. What time is it now—morning, afternoon, or evening?

Now, let's open our eyes and see how we did. *[Presenter 1 reads blackboard and checks off right answers.]*

ACTIVITY 6

OBJECTIVES: By the end of Activity 6, the children will have learned about "question mark" and "no" touches from people they know and about how to protect themselves from these touches.

Incest Sequence

Introduction

PRESENTER 1: Remember we said that people who sexually abuse kids can be strangers or people you know? In the play with the little boy and the Yard Teacher, the Yard Teacher was a stranger, pretending to be a friend, who tricked the boy into touch. Now we're going to talk about sexual abuse with some- one the child knows. Lots of times, someone the child knows and loves may try to force or trick the child into touch—a fam- ily friend, uncle, brother, cousin, grandparent, stepparent, or parent can force or trick a child into touch. *[For fourth- and fifth-graders:]* When someone in a kid's family sexually abuses a child, it is called "incest."

Purpose: To introduce and define the concept of incest

Father-Daughter Skit

PRESENTER 1: We're going to do a play now about a girl whose dad tries to trick her into touch. She's _____ (age of kids) years old. _____ (Presenter 2) will be the girl and I'll be the dad. It's Thursday night, and her mom goes to work/class (depending on school locality) every Thursday night. The girl is watching TV. Watch and see what happens.

[Two chairs in front/middle of semicircle. Girl sits in one, intently watching "TV" in front of her. Dad enters and sits on the chair beside her.]

Purpose: To illustrate concept of incest

Note: *The "work" can be changed to "class," depending on school locality.*

Presenter 1 = Dad

Presenter 2 = Girl

DAD: Hi Honey!

GIRL: Hi Dad. [*Doesn't look away from TV*]

DAD: This is our special night—our chance to spend time together while Mom's at work/school. Why don't you turn that TV off?

GIRL: Aw, Dad!

DAD: C'mon, I've got a great new game we can play. I can't tell you about it when the TV's on. You can watch TV anytime.

GIRL: Okay. [*Doesn't struggle too much about TV. Reaches out and turns it off.*]

DAD: That's more like it. [*Eases closer, putting arm around her.*] Come sit close to your dad. We don't get to spend much time together anymore.

GIRL: [*Smiling*] What's the new game?

Concept: Getting across the idea of teaching about sex

DAD: It's called the love game. I'm gonna teach you about love the way grown-ups do it. You're my special little girl. [*Strokes her hair gently.*] You play it like this. [*He places his hand on her thigh and girl's hand on his thigh. Strokes her leg.*]

GIRL: [*Looking uncomfortable, tries to move her hand away.*] I don't know, Dad.

Concept: Trust is used to manipulate daughter

DAD: It's okay. You can relax. This game is fun. Besides, I'm your dad. You can trust me. I wouldn't hurt you. [*Said softly and gently, while he brings her hand back to his leg, and holds her closer.*]

[*Girl seems hesitant, looks very uncomfortable and confused; no words, just a sigh.*]

Concept: Bribe

DAD: Tell you what. How'd you like to go rollerskating with me on Saturday in Golden Gate Park? [*Change name of park to suit your location.*]

GIRL: [*Smiles, brightens up a little*] Well, I'd like that!

DAD: [*Continuing to stroke her leg, says softly and seductively*] And I was thinking if you play this game with me, I'd buy you those roller skates we saw downtown.

GIRL: [*Excitedly*] You mean the ones with the pink laces?

DAD: Uh-huh! Just play this game with Dad. Oh, there's just one thing I forgot to mention. Don't tell anybody about this game. It's our little secret.

Concept: Secret

GIRL: I can't even tell Mom? [*Looks confused*] I don't know, Dad.

DAD: [*Firmly*] No, don't tell your mother! It would upset her. Besides you want those roller skates, don't you? [*Still has arm around her*]

GIRL: [*Nods reluctantly*] Uh-huh.

DAD: Then play this game with me, and keep it a secret! [*Girl looks down sadly. Dad hovers over her. Cut action.*]

Brainstorming with Class

PRESENTER 1:

a. How is this girl feeling? [*Three answers*] What kind of touch is this for the girl? How can you tell? [*Three answers*] Maybe it's a "?" touch because she loves her dad but she doesn't like the way he's touching her.

Purpose: To have children identify feelings of a victim

b. Did this girl get any funny feelings? When? [*Three to five answers. If children don't bring up bribes and secret, prompt for these.*]

Purpose: To identify funny feelings

c. Did she get a funny feeling when Dad said he'd take her rollerskating and buy her roller skates? What's that called? Yes. Dad was bribing her, to trick her into touch.

Concept: Bribes; Secrets

d. How about when Dad said, "Keep it a secret"? Did she have a funny feeling then? We think there are different kinds of secrets. One you keep for a little while, like for a surprise birthday party. That's an okay kind of secret. **There's another kind of secret that's not okay. When someone forces or tricks you into touching private**

Purpose: To apply safe-keeping skills to incest situations

Purpose: To identify support people for the child to tell

Purpose: To illustrate that first person told may not believe child

Presenter 1 = Mom

Presenter 2 = Girl

parts of your body or the other person's body and tells you not to tell ever, that's not the kind of secret you need to keep. Or if someone hurts you and tells you not to tell anyone, you can still tell. That's their secret, not yours. You can tell someone you trust. [*While talking, walk into middle of circle, to keep children's attention.*]

e. What can this girl do to keep herself safe?

f. When she first gets a funny feeling what can she say or do to keep safe? [*Three answers*]

g. What can she do later, so she can get the touch to stop? [*Three answers.*] Who could she tell? [*Someone will say "Mom".*] Yes, she could tell her mom, even though Dad said not to. And is it this girl's fault, if she couldn't stop the forced or tricked touch to private parts of her body? Even if she took the bribe? No, it's never the child's fault. Whose fault was it? That's correct. It was the dad's fault.

Mother-Daughter Skit

PRESENTER 2: This girl decided to tell her mother the next week, before she went to work/class. We're going to continue the play. This time _____ (Presenter 1) will be my mother. I'm going to try to tell my mom.

[*Two chairs in same place. Mom sits on one chair, preparing dinner. Girl approaches from the side.*]

GIRL: Mom, can I talk to you for a minute?

MOM: Uh-huh, but I'm in a hurry. I'm fixing your dinner and I've got to get to work/class. [*Keeps attention on dinner*]

GIRL: Mom, don't go to work/class tonight.

MOM: Don't be silly sweetie! I've got to go to work! You know we need the money! (Or: I've got to go to class! I've got a test tonight!) [*Says this half laughing, looks up at girl*]

GIRL: Well, it's just that last week when you went out, Dad wanted to play a funny game with me.

MOM: Isn't that nice that your daddy plays games. [*Pats her on the knee*] What a great guy, huh?

GIRL: But this was a love game, and he [*blurts it out*] touched me between my legs and all over. And he told me not to tell you!

MOM: What? How could you say that about your dad? I think you've been watching too much TV. It's putting wild ideas in your head. You know, you're lucky to have the dad you do. Now, go do your homework before dinner. And no TV tonight, and no more about those crazy games.

GIRL: [*Looks sad, and a little angry, sorry she brought it up; walks off with head down.*]

Brainstorming with Class

PRESENTER 1:

a. How does the girl feel now? [*Three answers*] Why does she feel sad, mad, afraid? [*Use class responses*]

b. What can she do now if the first person she tells doesn't believe her? [*Three answers*] Sometimes the first person a child tells about touches to private parts of the body may not believe the child. **But, it's important to tell and tell and tell, 'til someone does believe you!**

c. Who else can this girl tell? [*Three to five answers; someone will probably say "her friend." If not, prompt with, "Who could she tell at school?" Get them to think about resource people outside the family, such as principal, teachers, and friends.*]

Purpose: *To identify victim's feelings*

Concept: *People may not believe—even Mom. Keep telling.*

Friend Skit

[*Two chairs side by side. Presenters sit next to each other.*]

PRESENTER 2: We're going to do one more part of this play. This time _____ (Presenter 1) will be my best friend. Let's see what happens when I try to tell her.

GIRL: Hey, _____ (Presenter 1), can I stay over at your house tonight? I don't want to go home.

FRIEND: I think so. I have to ask my mom. What's up?

Purpose: *To illustrate the importance of telling someone else*

Presenter 1 = *Friend*

Presenter 2 = *Girl*

Concept: Children can keep not only themselves safe, but also can help friends keep safe.

GIRL: Tonight's the night Mom goes to work/class and Dad and I are home alone together.

FRIEND: I thought you liked being with your dad.

GIRL: I used to but he's been acting weird lately. Last week, he wanted to play a game and he touched me in my private parts and all over.

FRIEND: He shouldn't do that! Nobody has the right to touch you that way. That's called "sexual abuse" and it's against the law!

GIRL: But he made me promise not to tell, and said he'd buy me roller skates if I played the game. And I really wanted those skates. I think it's my fault.

FRIEND: It's not your fault! We learned about that in school. People came and said it's never the child's fault. I think you should tell somebody.

GIRL: Well I tried to tell my mom. But she didn't listen. I don't want anyone else to know. It's so embarrassing.

FRIEND: I know, but unless you tell, you won't be able to get him to stop and get some help.

GIRL: I don't know who else to tell.

FRIEND: How about my mom? She knows about things like that. Once last year I saw a flasher in the park, and she believed me. She helped me call the police. Maybe she could help you.

GIRL: I can't do it by myself. Will you go with me?

FRIEND: Sure. She's home now. Let's go! [*Both smile and walk off arm in arm.*]

Conclusion of Incest Sequence

PRESENTER 1:

    a. How is the girl feeling now? [*Three answers*] Why is she feeling happy, safe, relieved? [*Use class responses. Take three answers.*] Did her friend believe her? Did her friend make fun of her? Someone believed her. And now she's going to get help to stop the forced and tricked touch.

    b. Re-do of Role-Play with Helper (Optional, time allowing)

PRESENTER 1: Now we want to do this play one last time. Is there anyone who'd like to come up and be a friend to ___ (Presenter 2) and do what I did? [Presenter 1 picks helper.]

[Presenter 1 asks child how she will help _____ (Presenter 2) to tell. Then tells child he or she will be right next to her if child forgets. Presenter 2 may need to prompt child in re-do, if child freezes, by asking "Is it my fault?" "Who can I tell?" "Can we tell your mom?" and "Will you help me tell her?" At the end of the skit, applaud the child's efforts.]

PRESENTER 1: Now you know how to keep yourself and others safe from forced or tricked touch!

ACTIVITY 7

OBJECTIVES: By the end of Activity 7, the children will have learned about available sources of help in their community.

Resources

PRESENTER 1: If a child is sexually abused, he or she may have to tell someone, like a social worker or police officer. The child did not do anything wrong and is not in trouble, but it is important to tell, to get help so the abuse will stop.

PRESENTER 1: We're almost finished. We have two things we're going to leave with your teacher. He or she will give them to you after we go. The first is a certificate. It certifies that each one of you knows how to keep yourself and others safe from forced or tricked touch.

Purpose: To identify victim's feelings

Purpose: To give children practice helping a friend

Note: No preparation time is necessary for this re-do.

Purpose: *To give children resource numbers to call for help in their community*

Show Poster: *"Special Body Rights"*

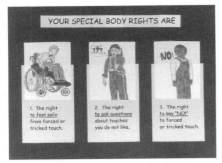

"SPECIAL BODY RIGHTS" POSTER

The second thing is called a "self-help card." On it are phone numbers you may need if you are or a friend is ever sexually abused. Keep it close to you in your pocket, purse, or backpack—just in case you need it. If you can't make the call by yourself, ask an adult you trust to help you. [*Explain all numbers to the class.*]

ACTIVITY 8

OBJECTIVES: By the end of Activity 8, children will have reviewed the basic concepts taught in Sessions 1 and 2.

Review

PRESENTER 2: Let's see how much you remember.

1. Who remembers what sexual abuse is? [*Take two answers. Then give our full definition of forced or tricked touch.*]

2. Let's say our special body rights together. [*Prompt with: You have . . . The right to feel . . . The right to say . . . The right to ask . . . . Show "Special Body Rights" poster.*]

3. What can you do to keep yourself safe if you get a "no" or "?" touch to private parts of your body or the other person's body? [*Make sure responses include: saying no; self-defense yell; keeping an arm's distance away; telling someone; running away; calling friends for help; making an excuse.*]

4. Who could you tell? [*Mom, Dad, uncles, aunts, grandparents, friends, teacher, cousin, brother, sister, principal, neighbors, police, etc.*]

5. If the child can't stop the forced or tricked touch to private parts of his or her body or someone else's body, is it the child's fault? It's always the fault of the person forcing or tricking the child into touch.

6. And if the child can't stop the forced or tricked touch, what can the child do afterwards to get help so that it doesn't happen again? [*Tell someone they trust.*]

7. Now we are going to sing "The Touching Song," and if you remember it, you can join us.

[*Hold up touching signs and sing.*]

ACTIVITY 9

OBJECTIVES: To give children another opportunity to clear up confusion about touches and to get help in stopping unwanted touches.

Conclusion/Private Time

PRESENTER 1: Now we're going to have Private Time. Like some of you did yesterday, you can talk to one of us, by yourself, about something that's on you mind. If you have a question or something you'd like to share about touches, please raise your hand. [*Presenter 2 writes names on board or paper.*]

PRESENTER 1: Thank you all very much. Once again, you've been a great class!

"THE TOUCHING SONG" WITH SIGNS

**"THE TOUCHING SONG" —
QUESTION MARK**

Appendix A:
Bibliography, Films, and Videos

Books for Children

It's My Body: A Book to Teach Young Children How to Resist Uncomfortable Touch

By Lory Freeman, illustrated by Carol Deach, 1982. Parenting Press, Inc. 7750 31st Ave., N.E., Suite 404, Seattle WA 98115. Cost: $3.00 (paperback) or $7.95 (hardcover).

Excellent, simple book for helping very young children be aware of the right to say "no" to uncomfortable touches. Reinforces idea that children don't have to let others touch them in ways they don't like. Appropriate for preschool children.

My Very Own Book about Me: A Personal Safety Book

By Joe Stowell and Mary Dietzel, 1982. Rape Crisis Resource Library, Lutheran Social Services of Washington, 1226 N. Howard, Spokane WA 99201. Cost: $3.00 plus postage and handling.

A very well written book, covering the concepts of kids' rights, being aware of feelings, comfortable and uncomfortable touches, how to get help, and other useful information. Several types of sexual abuse are described, including both boys and girls as victims, and family and nonfamily members as offenders. Appropriate for ages 4 to 10 years.

No More Secrets for Me

By Oralee Wachter, 1983. Little, Brown and Company, Trade Sales Department, 34 Beacon St., Boston MA 02106. Cost: $12.95 plus postage and handling.

Four well-written short stories illustrating such concepts as the right to say "no" to uncomfortable touches and how to get help when in an actual sexually abusive situation. Appropriate for elementary school children.

Private Zone: A Book Teaching Children Sexual Assault Prevention Tools

By Frances S. Dayee, illustrated by Marine Megale, 1982. The Charles Franklin Press, 18409 90th Ave. West, Edmonds WA 98020. Cost: $3.00 plus shipping and handling.

Straightforward, nonthreatening book for children. Written in storybook form; covers the concepts of the right to say "no" and how to get help. Teaches children that their genital area is theirs alone and not to be touched by others (except doctors and parents with the child's permission). Appropriate for ages 3 to 9 years.

Red Flag Green Flag People

By Joy Williams, 1980. Rape and Abuse Crisis Center, PO Box 1655, Fargo ND 58107. Cost: $4.00 plus postage and handling.

A coloring book which focuses mostly on the "dangerous stranger." Does not clearly define sexual abuse. Does show private parts of the body and helps children differentiate between touches that feel safe and touches that don't. Appropriate for ages 3 to 9.

Top Secret

By Jennifer Fay and Billie Jo Flerchinger, 1982. King County Rape Relief, Dept. D. M., 305 South 43rd, Renton WA 98055. (206) 226-5062.

Provides information about all forms of sexual assault, including incest and date rape. Appropriate for junior high and high school students.

A Very Touching Book

By Jan Hindman, 1983, McClure Hindman Books, PO Box 208, Durkee OR 97905. Cost: $9.95 plus postage and handling.

Much more explicit than most prevention books. Deals with learning names of body parts, secret touching, and how to get help. However, it uses "good" and "bad" to describe touches to private parts, which connotes judgment, and is not recommended by these authors. Appropriate for elementary school children.

What If . . . I Say No

By Jill Haddad and Lloyd Martin, 1981. M.H. Cap and Company, PO Box 3584, Bakersfield CA 93385.

Written in workbook form. Describes "good" and "bad" touches (not recommended by these authors) by both strangers and friends or relatives. Does not deal with improving the child's intuitive skills. Appropriate for elementary school children.

Books for Parents (On Prevention of Sexual Abuse)

Come Tell Me Right Away

By Linda Tschirhart Sanford, 1982. Ed-U Press, Inc. PO Box 583, Fayetteville NY 13066.

Well-written booklet (23 pages) explaining why children are vulnerable, and providing suggestions to parents on how to improve children's self-esteem and intuitive skills to decrease vulnerability. Note: Contact Ed-U Press for bulk orders of this pamphlet.

Fifty Ways to a Safer World

By Patricia Occhiuzzo Giggans and Barrie Levy, 1998. Seal Press, Seattle WA. Cost: $10.00 plus shipping and handling.

Excellent easy-to-read guide for parents of children and teens. Includes information on street safety, as well as personal safety with people known to the child. Encourages parents to become active in the movement to stop violence against women and children.

He Told Me Not to Tell

By Jennifer Fay, 1979. King County Rape Relief, 305 South 43rd, Renton WA 98055. (206) 226-0210. Call for bulk rates; may be out of print.

Excellent suggestions for parents or teachers on how to talk with children about sexual abuse, how to instill survival skills, and what to do if it is learned that a child has been abused. Brief, informative, and straightforward advice for preventing assault. (25 pages)

Keeping Kids Safe: Family Activity Booklet

By Pnina Tobin, 1997. Available from PMT Consultants, PO Box 12101, Berkeley CA 94712. (510) 547-5557. Cost: $10.00 plus shipping and handling.

Includes games and activities teaching prevention concepts for the whole family to do at home together. Appropriate for ages 3 to 10.

No More Secrets: Protecting Your Child from Sexual Assault

By Caren Adams and Jennifer Fay, 1981. Impact Publishers, PO Box 1094, San Luis Obispo CA 93406.

An expanded version of *He Told Me Not to Tell*. Provides parents and teachers with a wealth of excellent information on how to talk to children about sexual abuse, prevention games to play, indicators of potential dangerous situations, and how to help the child who has been victimized.

Protect Your Child from Sexual Abuse: A Parents' Guide

By Janice Hart-Rossi, 1984. Parenting Press, Inc. 7750 31st Avenue, N.E., Suite 404, Seattle WA 98115. Cost: $5.00 plus shipping and handling. Bulk discounts available.

A companion book to *It's My Body*. Gives parents and teachers many suggestions on how to approach concepts necessary to help children protect themselves. Gives a page-by-page guide for reading *It's My Body* with young children. Especially helpful for parents of preschool children. Offers activities to teach children prevention skills at home or at school. (59 pages)

The Silent Children: A Parent's Guide to the Prevention of Child Sexual Abuse

By Linda Tschirhart Sanford, 1980. McGraw-Hill, Garden City NY.

A comprehensive discussion of sexual abuse tailored specifically for parents. Includes a factual overview of molestation and incest, as well as sections on creating a family atmosphere conducive to nonvictim children, and on talking about sexual abuse with children. Both sections are extensive and concrete with suggested exercises for parents, and for parents and children together. A special closing section includes chapters written by Asian, Black, Hispanic, Native American, and single parents, as well as parents of developmentally disabled and physically disabled children, and parents of past victims.

Your Children Should Know

By Flora Colao and Tamar Hosansky. The Bobbs-Merrill Company, Inc. Indianapolis, IN/New York.

Using illustrations, teaches children self-defense and assertiveness techniques to ward off sexual assault. (160 pages)

Books for Adults
(On Sexual Abuse/Incest)

The Best Kept Secret: A History of Child Sexual Abuse

By Florence Rush, 1980. Prentice-Hall, Englewood Cliffs NJ.

A historical perspective provides significant insights into cultural contexts both for occurrence of sexual abuse and endurance of this phenomenon.

The Broken Taboo: Sex in the Family

By Blair and Rita Justice, 1979. Human Services Press, New York.

An overview of and treatment of the issue of incest. Case studies highlight family dynamics and the incest triangle. Suggestions for treatment and social change are included.

Conspiracy of Silence: The Trauma of Incest

By Sandra Butler, 1979. Bantam Books, New York.

A readable sociological overview of incest; its incidence, dynamics, and prevalent treatment. Contents include a review of pertinent literature and focus on the experiences of children, offenders, and mothers, often through first-person quotation. Concluding section concentrates on common professional responses to incest and their limitations. Accessible to lay and professional readers alike.

The Courage to Heal

By Ellen Bass and Laura Davis, 1994. Harper Perennial, New York.

A groundbreaking, comprehensive guide for women who were sexually abused as children. Warm and "user-friendly," this book charts the course of the healing process, with exercises, first-person stories, and clear narrative. Helpful for survivors and mental health workers alike.

Father's Day

By Katherine Brady, 1979. Seaview Books, New York.

An accessible narrative autobiography by a woman subjected to incest throughout her adolescence. Account dates from onset of assault through to the present and includes periods of self-destructive coping styles as well as healthy resolution.

Father-Daughter Incest

By Judith Lewis Herman, 1981. Harvard University Press, Cambridge MA.

A powerful feminist analysis of the problem of sexual abuse. Presents theory that patriarchal society causes and maintains father-daughter incest. Contains case histories and description of study done with L. Hirschman on adult survivors of child sexual abuse.

The Handbook of Clinical Intervention in Child Sexual Abuse

By Suzanne Sgroi, Editor, 1982. Lexington Books, Lexington MA/Toronto.

Excellent overview of treatment issues with sexually abused children, including individual and group work, art therapy, family dynamics, and sibling and mother issues. Also covers a multidisciplinary law enforcement team review of sexual abuse cases, and offers suggestions on how to start and evaluate a child sexual abuse intervention program.

I Know Why the Caged Bird Sings

By Maya Angelou, 1971. Bantam Books, New York.

In her autobiography, Ms. Angelou includes a moving account of her own sexual assault by a family member. Portrays the expression of her responses at the time and the effect of her mother's support.

If I Should Die Before I Wake

By Michelle Morris, 1984. Dell Books, New York.

A moving and harrowing account of one teenage girl's experience of father-daughter incest, from age 5 on. Effectively and sensitively portrays the trauma, self-hatred, and ambivalence toward the offender felt by many victims of sexual abuse.

Kiss Daddy Goodnight: A Speak Out on Incest

By Louise Armstrong, 1979. Simon and Schuster, New York.

An often grueling collection of letters and interviews with incest victims across the country, solicited and assembled by a survivor of incest. Content includes sometimes detailed accounts of assault experiences, as well as some reports of conflict in resolution of after-effects. Especially important series of letters from "Annabelle" that demonstrates both the power and detriment of denial as a coping mechanism.

Sexual Assault of Children and Adolescents

By Ann Wolbert Burgess, N. Groth, L. Holstrom, and S. Sgroi, 1978. Jossey-Bass, San Francisco.

A national needs assessment plus fourteen chapters encompassing offenders (patterns, guidelines for assessment and management, issues referencing the adolescent offender); victims (complicating factors, pressure and secrecy, divided loyalty); and services (guidelines for intervention and assessment, diagnostic-therapeutic-protection issues, interviewing victims, police investigation, court process, coordinated community treatment).

Sexually Victimized Children

By David Finkelhor, 1979. The Free Press (MacMillan Paperback), New York.

A study of sexually victimized children with an emphasis on incest. Presents theories and case histories of children's sexual experiences with adults, discusses traumatic effects of sexual abuse on children, and offers suggestions for dealing with this societal problem.

Films for Children

No More Secrets

O.D.N. Productions, Inc.,1980. 74 Varick St., Ste. 304, New York NY 10013 (13 minutes, color, animated in parts)

Excellent prevention film for ages 7 through 12. Four children discuss uncomfortable experiences they have had with family members regarding sexual abuse. After each problem is presented, children brainstorm solutions with each other. They encourage each other to say "no" and to tell a trusted adult. Suggestions from peers provide an effective way to promote prevention.

Some Secrets Should Be Told

By Susan Linn, 1982 Family Information Systems and Resource Communications, Inc. (12 min., color)

A very sensitive conversation among two puppets—a duck and a lion—and ventriloquist Susan Linn about sexual abuse. Presentation is direct and supportive and encourages children to tell a trusted adult. Suitable for preschool and early elementary school children.

What Tado?

A J. Gary Mitchell Film. M. T. I. Teleprograms, Inc. 3710 Commercial Ave., Northbrook IL 60062. (800) 323-5343.

Geared toward preschool and early elementary school children, this film uses puppets and actors to illustrate basic concepts of sexual abuse prevention. CAUTION: the section concerning "lures" is problematic: scenes such as a man pretending to be a policeman may be more misleading and frightening than instructive for young children.

Who Do You Tell?

A J. Gary Mitchell Film. M. T. I. Teleprograms, Inc., 3710 Commercial Ave., Northbrook IL 60062. (800) 323-5343. (11 minutes, color, animated in parts)

General prevention film for children. Uses film clips and animated segments to instruct children to rely on their family and community support systems when problems arise that are too big to handle by themselves. Treats problems such as spousal abuse, physical abuse, and sexual abuse by strangers and people known to the child—along with what to do in case of a fire or if someone gets lost—in a nonthreatening, upbeat manner. Suitable for ages 5 to 11.

Videotapes

No Easy Answers

Resolution, Inc., One Mill St., Burlington VT 05401.

Illusion Theater's theatrical presentation for adolescents on video. Video and guide assist in prevention of abuse by providing an overview of various types of sexual abuse, with discussion about the individual and social factors that perpetuate sexual abuse.

Strong Kids, Safe Kids

Paramount Home Video, 5555 Melrose Ave., Hollywood CA 90038 (43 minutes, color, animated in parts)

Home video on sexuality and sexual abuse prevention for parents and children to watch together. Uses video graphics, familiar cartoon characters, TV personalities, and experts in the field to highlight sexual abuse prevention skills. Shows children from San Francisco singing "The Touching Song," doing the self-defense yell, and saying "no!" Emphasizes the importance of telling someone you trust. CAUTION: somewhat unfocused and didactic in parts, but a generally effective teaching tool. Appropriate for preschool and elementary school children. However, some of the material is too sophisticated for preschoolers, and some too oversimplified for older children. Parents should use their own discretion.

Touch

Resolution, Inc. One Mill St., Burlington VT 05401.

Describes the Illusion Theater's continuum of touch—nurturing, confusing, and exploitive—in a balanced and nonthreatening way, while giving children and parents clear definitions of "sexual abuse," ideas for prevention, and protection skills.

When Romance Turns to Rape

By Sherri Patterson, C.L.A.S.S. Project, 116 4th St., San Rafael CA 94901.

Highlights key issues in date rape, focusing on clear ways teens can communicate, set sexual limits, and assert themselves.

Films for Adults

A Time for Caring: The School's Response to the Sexually Abused Child

A Profile Film, Lawren Productions, Mendocino CA.
(28 minutes, color)

Although written for public school staffs, the information could provide an excellent training tool for childcare personnel as well.

Breaking Silence

By Theresa Tollini. Future Educational Films, Film Distribution Center, 1028 Industry Dr., Seattle WA 98188. (206) 575-1575. (58 minutes, color) For rental and purchase. Also available in video.

Absorbing and moving documentary on incest, intertwining first-hand accounts from survivors, commentary from mental health professionals, and prevention strategies to deal with the problem. *Keeping Kids Safe* early childhood curriculum is highlighted. Excellent for training laypeople and professionals alike.

Incest: The Victim Nobody Believes

A J. Gary Mitchell Film. The J. Gary Mitchell Film Company, 163 Tunstead Ave., San Anselmo CA 94960 (21 minutes, color). Also in video.

Filmed conversation among three survivors of incest, each exploring, reacting to, and dealing with her childhood experiences in her own way. Powerful plea for sexual abuse prevention programs.

Audiotapes

"The Touching Song" and "The Funny Feelings Song"

By Pnina Tobin. Available through PMT Consultants, PO Box 12101, Berkeley CA 94712. Cost: $8.00 per tape, plus shipping and handling.

These songs can be used separately, or with early childhood and elementary curricula to reinforce the concepts of positive, negative, and confusing touches; funny feelings; and ways children can keep safe from unwanted touches.

Appendix B:
Handouts for Parents and Teachers

Handouts for parents and teachers are a very important addition to parent and teacher meetings. They provide pertinent information on the program, answer critical questions regarding child abuse, and offer resources parents can refer to when necessary.

When developing material for parents, it is essential to include the following:

Content:

- Information on your child abuse prevention program

- A few key facts about child sexual abuse

- General indicators of the child sexual abuse of children and teens

- Local resources and reporting information for child abuse victims and their families (resources can also include help for related problems)

- Prevention strategies for parents to use at home

- Bibliography of books, videos, and films for children and adults on the subject of child sexual abuse

Format:

Your information for parents and teachers should be designed with busy adults' needs in mind.

- All information should be concise and to the point.

- It should be printed on colorful paper to attract attention.

- The print should be large enough to be easily readable.

- It should be written in a style that is accessible to all parents, regardless of their level of education.

- Translated material should be provided as needed.

Appendix C:
Teacher/Parent Follow-Up Exercise

(To Use with Children)

1. List the three **basic body safety rights:**

   a.

   b.

   c.

2. List the **three kinds of touches:**

   a.

   b.

   c.

3. List two things adults may use to bribe children into forced or tricked touches:

   a.

   b.

4. List two skills children may use to keep safe:

   a.

   b.

5. Who would you tell if someone tried to force you or trick you into touching?

   a.

   b.

6. If the first person a child tells about forced or tricked touching cannot help the child, what should he or she do?

7. Is sexual abuse (forced or tricked touch) ever the child's fault?

[See also the *Keeping Kids Safe: Family Activity Booklet,* available for $15 plus postage from PMT Consultants, PO Box 12101, Berkeley CA 94712. Phone: (510) 547-5557.]

Appendix D:
Sample Class Participation Form

PERMISSION SLIP

Dear Parent,

With your permission, your child will be invited to participate in the *Keeping Kids Safe* Program to be held at _____ school. If you approve, she or he will be involved in two 1-hour teaching sessions on _____ (date) and _____ (date).

Parents and other responsible adults want to protect children from those who might harm them, but no child can be supervised 24 hours a day. The *Keeping Kids Safe* Program will teach your child ways he or she can reduce the likelihood of being sexually abused and ways to get help from others if needed.

So that we may respect your wishes, please indicate below whether you *want your child to participate in this program.* Please sign the following statement, tear it off, and have your child bring it to her or his teacher.

If you have any questions, please call _____ (your agency name) at _____ (phone).

Thank you,
Director, Local Prevention Program

To: Principal

School Name:_____

School Address:_____

____ **Yes, I would like my child to participate in the *Keeping Kids Safe* Program.**

____ **No, I do not want my child to participate in the *Keeping Kids Safe* Program.**

Please indicate your preference, sign the form, and ask your child to return it to his or her teacher.

_____

(Your signature and date)

_____

(Name of child)

Appendix E:
Sample Class Participation Form— Spanish Version

PERMISO PARA PARTICIPACION

Estimados Padres:

Su niño o niña ha sido invitado para participar en un programa especiál de ayuda própia para el estudiante (*Keeping Kids Safe* Program). Él o ella tomará parte en dos sesiones, de enseñanza de una hora cada una: _____ y _____.

    Nosotros, como padres, queremos proteger a nuestros hijos contra personas que les puedan abusar. Es imposible supervisarlos 24 horas del día. Nuestro proyecto les enseñara a los niños modos de protegerse a si mismos contra abusos sexuales. También les enseñaremos como pueden recibir ayuda si han sido abusados o asaltados.

    Si ústed tiene alguna pregunta haga el favor de llamar al número de teléfono

_____

Muchísimas grácias,

Director, Local Prevention Program

- -

To: Principal

School Name:_____

School Address:_____

_____ **Sí, quiero que mi niño o mi niña asista a las dos horas de ensenanza en como prevenir abuso sexual, el programa dirigido por the *Keeping Kids Safe* Program.**

_____ **No, no quiero que mi niño o mi niña asista a las dos horas de ensenanza en como prevenir abuso sexual, el programa dirigido por the *Keeping Kids Safe* Program**

Please indicate your preference, sign the form, and ask your child to return it to his or her teacher.

_____

(Nombre del padre, madre, guardián)   (fetcha)

_____

(Nombre de niño o niña cuarto)

Appendix F:
"The Touching Song"

Chorus
There are three kinds of touches, this we know—
A "heart," a "question mark," and "no."
"No" means "stop,"
"Heart" means "go,"
and "question mark" means "I don't know."

Verse 1
Now if I tickle you and you say "no"
And I don't stop, where should you go?
You could go and tell somebody you know
And keep very safe from the tickle-o.

Verse 2

What if a bully pushes you down
And there's nobody else around?
You can run for help because, you see,
That's a "no" touch, we all agree.

Verse 3

You see Aunt Janie only once a year
And when she finally does appear,
She gives you a "heart" touch, that's very clear.
We can see you grin from ear to ear!

Verse 4
When you sit on his lap, your Uncle Sam
Is sweet and tender as a lamb.
But if "lamb-Sam" touches you where you don't like,
You can tell him to "go take a hike!"

Appendix G:
"The Funny Feelings Song"

Verse

A funny feeling's a voice inside you.
It's there to help you.
It's there to guide you.
And if you listen, a voice will go,
"Uh-oh, better say no,"
"Uh-oh, better say no."

Chorus

Better say "no"
Better say "no."
And if you listen,
A voice will go,
"Uh-oh, better say no."

©1983 by Pnina Tobin

[Words and music to "The Touching Song" and "The Funny Feelings Song" are available on cassette tape and may be purchased using the ordering form found on the next page.

CHILD ABUSE PREVENTION

check box

I'm Somebody—A Child Sexual Abuse Prevention Manual for Children with Disabilities.
P. Tobin, L. Rifkin, C. Carpenter ....$30 + $3 shipping ☐

Keeping Kids Safe—A Child Sexual Abuse Prevention Manual.
P. Tobin and S. Levinson Kessner...$25 + $3 shipping each ☐

Keeping Kids Safe—Family Activity Booklet ....$15 each + $2 shipping ☐

Posters (14) for use with *Keeping Kids Safe* & *I'm Somebody* Programs.......$395 + $45 shipping ☐

Preventing Sexual Abuse. Videotape
P. Folger ....$15 + $2 shipping ☐

Puppets—Child-Size (Purple, Yellow, Green,
Safety Friend) ....$550/set of 4 puppets + $25 shipping ☐

"The Touching Song" and "The Funny Feelings Song" audiocassette
P. Tobin..$8 + $2 shipping ☐

PARENTING

Taking a Second Look at Roles, Supermom to the Rescue,
and *Filling the Void—Releasing Supermom Patterns.* Set of articles from
MOMMA Newspaper for Single Mothers. ....3 article set $5 + $1 shipping ☐

TOTAL _____

Please send this form plus your check (including shipping charges) to:
PMT Consultants, PO Box 12101, Berkeley, CA 94712

Outside U.S., please add $10 to shipping cost.

Name _____

Address _____

City, State, Zip _____

Phone _____

E-mail _____

Child Sexual Abuse Prevention ■ Disabilities and Abuse ■ Parenting Skills ■ Women in Transition
PO Box 12101, Berkeley, CA 94712 (510) 547-5557 fax: (510) 547-5560

GROW: Growth and Recovery Outreach Workbooks

by Wendy Deaton, MFCC, with Kendall Johnson, Ph.D.

A creative, child-friendly program designed for use with elementary school children, filled with original exercises to foster healing, self-understanding and optimal growth.

These popular workbooks are designed for helping children who have experienced trauma. Each has friendly but neutral artwork and plenty of space in which to write and draw. With one-on-one support and feedback, the child works through the exercises in the book, which are balanced between writing and drawing, left and right brain, thinking and feeling. All exercises follow a therapeutic sequence: creating an alliance, debriefing traumatic memories, exploring delayed reactions, teaching coping strategies and integrating the experience.

Each workbook comes with a removable four-page guide containing an overview of the workbook and page-by-page explanations of each activity. The explanations are cross-referenced to *Trauma in the Lives of Children* (see below).

Workbooks for children ages 9–12:

I AM A SURVIVOR — for children who have survived a natural disaster such as a flood, tornado, hurricane, fire or earthquake.

I SAW IT HAPPEN — for children who have witnessed a traumatic event such as a shooting at school, a frightening accident or other violence.

NO MORE HURT — provides a safe place for children who have been physically or sexually abused to explore and share their feelings.

LIVING WITH MY FAMILY — helps children traumatized by domestic violence and family fights to identify and express their fears.

SOMEONE I LOVE DIED — for children who have lost a loved one and are dealing with grief, loss and helplessness.

A SEPARATION IN MY FAMILY — for working with children whose parents are separating or have already separated or divorced.

DRINKING AND DRUGS IN MY FAMILY — for children who have family members who engage in regular alcohol or substance abuse.

Workbooks for children ages 6–10:

MY OWN THOUGHTS AND FEELINGS (for Girls) or MY OWN THOUGHTS AND FEELINGS (for Boys) — for exploring early symptoms of depression, low self-esteem, family conflict, maladjustment, and nonspecific dysfunction.

MY OWN THOUGHTS AND FEELINGS ON STOPPING THE HURT — helps communication with young children who may have suffered physical or sexual abuse.

Wendy Deaton, MFCC, has a counseling practice specializing in families and children. **Kendall Johnson, Ph.D.,** is a mentor teacher and crisis management expert who consults with school districts throughout the U.S.

**All single workbooks: $9.95
10-pack: $70.00**

Workbook Library (one of each workbook–10 total) Special: $75.00

For bulk discounts and additional ordering information, please call Hunter House at (800) 266-5592

Trauma in the Lives of Children: *Crisis and Stress Management Techniques for Counselors, Teachers, and Other Professionals*

by Kendall Johnson, Ph.D.   *Revised Second Edition*

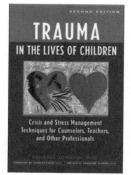

Parental separation, violence in the home, a shooting at school, the death of a loved one—all these events can affect a child's development, health, school performance, family interactions and self-esteem. *Trauma in the Lives of Children* explains how children react to specific types of trauma, how to recognize and address a traumatized child and what professionals and families can do to help traumatized children. The expanded second edition covers the nationwide movement toward School Crisis Response Teams and the use of EMDR as a posttrauma treatment modality. A special chapter on trauma prevention helps schools and families prepare for crises.

Paperback $19.95 ... 352 pp. ... 2 illus. ... 16 tables

For information on Kendall Johnson, Ph.D., please see above

KEEP SAFE! 101 Ways to Enhance Your Safety & Protect Your Family

by Donna Wells, M.Ed., MPA, and Bruce Morris, J.D.

This compact book presents effective practices for preventing violence and avoiding dangerous situations through forethought and planning. These pro-active guidelines can be incorporated into daily routines to make safety a habit. Sections focus on key life areas: at Home; in School; in Your Community; at Work; at Play; and On the Road.

Much of the book focuses on children's safety. Specific sections address keeping involved in children's lives, along with a comprehensive chapter on school safety.

Paperback $12.95 ... 192 pp. ... 30 b/w illus.

Helping Your Child Through Your Divorce

by Florence Bienenfeld, Ph.D.

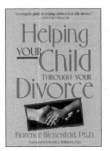

This practical guide encourages divorcing parents to focus on what is best for their child and to forge a new alliance —as parent partners who are no longer marriage partners. Includes examples of model agreements and strategies for dealing with common problems such as visits during holidays. Drawings by children of divorcing parents poignantly illustrate the anger and hurt that children feel as a result of being pulled between parents.

Paperback $14.95 ... Second Edition ... 224 pp. ... 37 illus. ... 4 charts

Human Rights for Children

by the Amnesty International Human Rights for Children Committee

This curriculum encourages the development of self-worth and multicultural awareness. It is organized in ten sections, one for each principle of the U.N. Declaration of the Rights of the Child. Each section offers activities and exercises in social science and history, science and math, current events, creative arts and physical education. Now you can promote peace and respect by helping children develop an awareness of their rights and the rights of others.

With illustrations by Marsha Sinetar

Spiral bound $14.95 ... 80 pp. ... 13 illus. ... Ages 3–12

When Violence Begins at Home: *A Comprehensive Guide to Understanding and Ending Domestic Abuse*   by K. J. Wilson, Ed.D.

With understanding and empathy, this guide to domestic violence addresses the needs of multiple audiences, including battered women of various ages and backgrounds, teenaged victims of dating violence, educators, community leaders, legal officials and even the batterers themselves. A comprehensive listing of local and national resources directs affected people to information and an extensive network of people who can help.

Paperback $19.95 ... Hardcover $29.95 ... 416 pp. ... 2 illus.

I Can Make My World a Safer Place

A Kid's Book about Stopping Violence

by Paul Kivel • Illustrations and games by Nancy Gorrell

This book for kids ages 6–11 shows what children can do to find alternatives to violence in their lives. Kivel explains public danger (gangs, fights and drug-related violence) and private danger (sexual assault and domestic violence) and gives suggestions for staying safe. Simple text and activities such as mazes and word searches encourage young readers to think about and promote peace. Activism is discussed, using examples such as Cesar Chavez and Julia Butterfly. The multicultural drawings by Nancy Gorrell are playful and engaging, guiding the reader, reinforcing the text and making difficult ideas easier to understand.

Paul Kivel is an accomplished trainer, speaker and author and has been an innovative leader in the field of violence prevention for more than 20 years. **Nancy Gorrell** is a child-care worker and artist.

Paperback $11.95 ... 96 pp. ... 90 illus.

Magical Mandala Coloring Books

42 Mandala Patterns Coloring Book
42 Indian Mandalas Coloring Book
42 Seasonal Mandalas Coloring Book
by Wolfgang Hund and Monika Helwig

All books: Paperback $9.95ea ... 96 pages ... 42 b/w drawings

Mandalas represent wholeness and life. Their designs contain themes and patterns taken from geometry, nature and folk art. Made up of simple elements, yet often marvelously complex, they fascinate children and adults alike. Mandalas have been found on the walls of prehistoric caves, in ancient tapestries and stained glass windows and in the artistic expression of people all over the world.

These three books of mandalas can be used anywhere—all you need is a set of colored pens, pencils or crayons.

Mandala patterns—circles of life

These mandalas are drawn from the entire world of design and nature, mixing traditional and modern themes. They include nature elements and animals and are a perfect introduction to the joy of coloring mandalas.

Indian mandalas—traditional household and village art

These mandalas are based on ornamental patterns created in India. Traditionally made of colored rice powder, flower petals, leaves or colored sand, they are used to decorate homes, temples and meeting places.

Seasonal mandalas—windows into nature's cycles

The mandalas in this book mix Eastern and Western themes and include fruit, flowers, leaves and snowflakes, while more whimsical patterns include bunnies and spring chicks, jack-o-lanterns, Christmas scenes and New Year's noisemakers.

SmartFun Activity Books —*for ages 4 and up*

These activity books encourage imagination, social interaction and self-expression in children. Age levels, times of play and group size are indicated for each game. Most games are noncompetitive; none of them require special skills or training; all participants, regardless of their level of physical coordination, can enjoy them. The series is widely used in schools, day-care centers, clubs and camps.

All books: Paperback $12.95 ...Spiral bound $17.95
160–192 pp. ... 30–45 illus.

101 Music Games for Children
Fun and Learning with Rhythm and Song
by Jerry Storms

Using tapes or CDs, children and adults get to play listening games, concentration games, musical quizzes and more.

101 More Music Games for Children
New Fun and Learning with Rhythm and Song **by Jerry Storms**

The songs and games from many cultures include rhythm games, dance and movement games and musical projects.

101 Dance Games for Children
Fun and Creativity with Movement
by Paul Rooyackers

Children can interact and express themselves in creative fantasies and without words in meeting and greeting games, story dances, party dances and more.

101 Drama Games for Children
Fun and Learning with Acting and Make-Believe **by Paul Rooyackers**

Drama games are not staged plays but a form in which children explore their minds and world through sensory games, pantomimes, puppets, masks and costumes.

101 Movement Games for Children
Fun and Learning with Playful Moving
by Huberta Wiertsema

These games teach children to use their bodies for expression and include variations on old favorites such as "Red Rover, Red Rover," and new games such as "Mirroring," and "Moving Joints."

ORDER FORM

NAME _____

ADDRESS _____

CITY/STATE _____ ZIP/POSTCODE _____

PHONE _____ COUNTRY (outside of U.S.) _____

TITLE	QTY	PRICE	TOTAL
Keeping Kids Safe (paperback)		@ $24.95	
Keeping Kids Safe (spiral)		@ $29.95	

Prices subject to change without notice

Please list other titles below:

		@ $	
		@ $	
		@ $	
		@ $	
		@ $	
		@ $	
		@ $	

Check here to receive our book catalog ☐ FREE

Shipping Costs:
First book: $3.00 by book post ($4.50 by UPS, Priority Mail, or to ship outside the U.S.)
Each additional book: $1.00
For rush orders and bulk shipments call us at (800) 266-5592

TOTAL	_____
Less discount @_____%	(_____)
TOTAL COST OF BOOKS	_____
Calif. residents add sales tax	_____
Shipping & handling	_____
TOTAL ENCLOSED	_____

Please pay in U.S. funds only

☐ Check ☐ Money Order ☐ Visa ☐ MasterCard ☐ Discover

Card # _____ Exp. date _____

Signature _____

Complete and mail to:
Hunter House Inc., Publishers
PO Box 2914, Alameda CA 94501-0914
Orders: (800) 266-5592 email: ordering@hunterhouse.com
Phone (510) 865-5282 Fax (510) 865-4295
☐ Check here to receive our book catalog

KKS-01/2002